Sheila Walsh

"I get calls every day from people who want to know how to hold on to heaven when it seems that the very powers of hell itself are tearing at them.... They want to know, 'Where are you God?' They know Satan is there. And Satan seems to be winning."

HOLDING ON TO HEAVEN WITH HELL ON YOUR BACK

Thomas Nelson Publishers
Nashville

❖ *A Janet Thoma Book* ❖

Published in Nashville, Tennessee, by Thomas Nelson, Inc., and distributed in Canada by Lawson Falle, Ltd., Cambridge, Ontario.

Printed in the United States of America.

Scripture quotations unless otherwise noted are from *The Everyday Bible, New Century Version*, copyright © 1987 by Worthy Publishing, Fort Worth, TX 76137. Used by permission.

Those noted KJV are from the King James Version of the Bible.

Those noted NIV are from the *Holy Bible: New International Version*. Copyright © 1973, 1978, 1984 by the International Bible Society. Used by permission of Zondervan Bible Publishers.

Those noted TLB are from *The Living Bible*, copyright © 1971 by Tyndale House Publishers, Wheaton, IL. Used by permission.

Library of Congress Cataloging-in-Publication Data

Walsh, Sheila, 1956–
    Holding onto heaven with hell on your back / Sheila Walsh.
      p.   cm.
    Includes bibliographical references.
    ISBN 0-8407-7485-0
    1. Christian life—1960–   2. Walsh, Sheila, 1956–   / I. Title.
II. Title: Holding onto heaven with hell on your back.
BV4501.2.W327   1990
248.4—dv20   90-38327
                                                      CIP

Printed in the United States of America
1 2 3 4 5 6 7 — 95 94 93 92 91 90

This book is dedicated with all my love to my husband Norman. We have traveled some rough seas together, but ours is a strong ship.

CONTENTS

O N E

It Wasn't Supposed to Be This Way

When life doesn't make sense anymore
because all of hell seems to be on our backs,
we can give up, or we can remember who Jesus really is
and that no matter how dark it gets,
He is worth it all.

Somewhere in the distance I could hear the radio. It was playing an annoyingly happy song, completely inappropriate at 6:00 A.M. I lay there and considered my options:

"Sheila has been struck by a mysterious virus and is unable to appear on the '700 Club' today."

Tempting? Yes, but living with my conscience would be even harder than getting up, so . . . I slid out of bed and into the shower. As I dressed I could hear Norman's oblivious snores coming from the depth of the cozy down comforter I had just vacated. I felt tempted to wake him for an early morning Bible study, but, fortunately, mercy—and better judgment—prevailed.

As I pulled out of the driveway my thoughts turned to a telephone conversation that I'd had the day before.

A man of about sixty years of age called the "700 Club" to

ask for help. I could tell that he was embarrassed and anxious about turning to a young woman for advice, but something made him call.

"I watched your program yesterday," he said. "You seem to care about people. I'm really sorry to take up your time, but I'm so unhappy."

I tried to reassure him that I was happy to talk with him and that I was a friend.

He told me that he'd been married for thirty-six years and now he'd ruined it all. I sat quietly praying for wisdom and let him continue.

"You see, I really love my wife, but years ago I had a fling, nothing much, really, just a stupid fling. It lasted only a few weeks." As he continued his story, I could feel the anguish in his voice. He stopped for a moment.

"Does your wife know about this?" I asked.

"Well, you see, that's just it," he said. "I gave my life to God a few weeks ago, and I wanted to put things right. So I told my wife and asked her to forgive me, and now she's gone. She's gone." He began to cry bitterly, and I wished I could reach across the telephone miles and comfort him.

"It wasn't supposed to be this way," he said.

As I pulled into the driveway at CBN, his words rang in my ears. *It wasn't supposed to be this way.* Everywhere I went, it seemed I heard those words.

Earlier that same week I had a similar conversation. It was about 6:00 in the evening, and I stood in a long line at the supermarket, waiting to pay for our evening meal. A lady of about forty years began to ring up my purchases.

"I watch you every night, Sheila," she said. "I pray with you, too, but it doesn't seem to be working."

She went on to tell me that her husband had left her for a younger woman. Her son was involved with drug dealing and petty theft.

"I'm also quite ill," she said. "I pray with you every day, and I wonder why God doesn't answer my prayers. I try to have enough faith, but I just don't seem to be winning."

It wasn't supposed to be this way.

Following our usual pre-broadcast briefing, Pat Robertson and I went to Studio Seven to tape the "700 Club." It was five minutes to ten. He asked who I was interviewing that day on my new show, "Heart to Heart," which follows the "Club." I began to tell him about Darrell Gilyard, but then the cameras rolled and it was five, four, three, two . . . "Thank you, ladies and gentlemen, and welcome to the '700 Club.'"

After our "700 Club" broadcast, I immediately went into my interview with Darrell Gilyard. There was a buzz around CBN about my guest. I'd been told by several people who had seen him on Jerry Falwell's program that he was an unusual man of God. I knew very little about him as he took his seat beside me on the "Heart to Heart" set, but his story left an indelible mark on my heart.

When he was nine months old, his mother and father stood on the steps of a total stranger's home and gave their son away. This young black couple begged the older black woman who answered the door to care for their child for just a little while, but they never came back. So Darrell was raised by a godly, caring woman, who daily taught him about Jesus.

When he was just seven years old, she called him to her bedside. "Son, I'm dying. I'm poorer than your parents were, so I've nothing much to leave you." With that she thrust her old *Good News for Modern Man* Bible into his hands and said, "I leave you Jesus."

Darrell was passed from foster home to foster home. He was longing for love, trying to hold onto his faith.

When he was fourteen years old, he found himself out on the streets. He had no name, no family he knew, no one who

11

cared if he lived or died. He made his bed under a bridge, selling cans and bottles to make enough to eat. He kept going to school, washing his one set of clothes in the river. At night he would sit under the light of a convenience store to do his homework. He was determined not to be a loser.

But there were plenty of cold nights when he lifted his face to the sky and asked God, "Why?" Was it too much to ask for a bed? For a friend? For someone to say goodnight to? As he stood there, a solitary figure against the night, he knew *it wasn't supposed to be this way.*

Why Does Satan Seem to Be Winning?

The man on the phone, the checker at the supermarket, the boy under the bridge—they all asked the questions that pound in my brain, each one a lead weight. Every day those same kinds of questions come in over the phone lines at CBN from people who listen and watch and wonder, "Can I make it? Can I hold onto heaven when hell itself is tearing at my back?" These people want to know whether God is really there and whether He really cares. They have no trouble knowing Satan is there—and Satan seems to be winning. That's why they ask:

"Where is God when my life is so full of hurt?"

"Why did I get laid off when my neighbor, who hasn't been to church twice in the past five years, gets promoted?"

"Why did my husband leave me for *her?*"

"Why doesn't God heal me . . . or my spouse . . . or my child?"

Why? Why? Why?

"Why?" is the question that eats at many of us. Just when we think we've finally understood God, He does something that makes no sense, no sense at all to us.

As I began to scan my Bible, looking for light and hope to

answer the questions of so many, I fell back into step with my old friend Job. The book of Job has always fascinated me. I've heard innumerable sermons on it and read wonderful books on it, but every time I dig my shovel in, there is always fresh soil.

As Job's familiar story opens, we learn that he was a good man, a loyal husband, and a caring father. He was also a friend of God's.

The scene shifts to the courts of heaven. We see the angels coming before God, and Satan was among them.

God called Satan's attention to His servant Job. "No one else on earth is like him," said the Lord. "He is an honest man and innocent of any wrong. He honors God and stays away from evil" (Job 1:8).

But Satan wasn't impressed. "Of course, he's a good man. He's no fool. He loves You because it pays to love You. Take away all his fringe benefits, and You've lost Yourself one very selfish human being."

But God didn't agree. He said, "You're wrong. Job is a friend of Mine. Even if he lost everything, he'd still love Me." In a sense, God staked His reputation on the life of one man. God gave Satan permission to tear Job's life apart. Job lost everything. His sons, daughters, and servants were killed and his vast herds of livestock stolen.

True to God's prediction, Job stood fast. In the midst of his sorrow, he declared, "The Lord gives and the Lord takes away. Blessed be the name of the Lord."[1]

Not long afterward, God and Satan met again, and the Lord said, "Well, what do you think about Job now? Didn't I tell you there was nobody on earth like him? He was ruined for no reason, but he only praised My Name and continues to be without blame."

Satan sneered and retorted with a proverb often used by tradesmen of Job's time: "One skin for another! Of course,

Job was willing to give up the lives of his animals, his servants, and his children, *but what about his own skin?* Every human is selfish. Why don't you let me touch Job's body and ruin his health? A man can live without his children. A man can live without his wealth, but cause him personal pain, and he'll curse You to Your face!"

"All right then," God replied. "Touch Job's body, but you cannot kill him."

And so Satan afflicted Job from the top of his head to the bottom of his feet with the most painful kinds of boils and sores. In incredible misery, Job sat on a heap of ashes, scraping his sores with a piece of broken pottery, but he never said a word against God.

What does Job's story have to say to you and me? Is it a dangerous thing to fall into the hands of God? Can He be trusted? What does it really mean to be His servant and His child? Why would God stand back and allow the enemy to bruise His children? Why would God seem to turn a deaf ear to our prayers? Why would He allow our mortal enemy to toy with us?

I've often wondered how Job prayed during those seven days and seven nights when the sky was like brass and nobody seemed to be listening. I wonder whether Job might at least have been tempted to mutter, *Lord, it wasn't supposed to be this way.*

No, a lot of life wasn't supposed to be this way, but it is. And when our prayers bounce off the ceiling and land right back in our faces, we feel guilty for asking why. After all, Christians are supposed to have all the answers. Theoretically, we are the ones who can deal with life because we have a powerful and loving God Who answers our prayers and gives the victory. In reality, God often seems to answer with a "No," or a "Please wait. My plan is in place; just trust Me."

I believe that when we base our faith on apparent answered prayer, getting the solutions to our problems *right now,* we're in real trouble. If we mistake God's silence for indifference, we are the most miserable of people. If we give up when we no longer understand, we reject His caring, steadfast love and cut ourselves off from our only real hope.

Satan, of course, is sitting back hoping that that's exactly what will happen—that we will give up, quit, and pack it in. That's why Satan slithers up to a sixty-year-old heartbroken man whose wife has just left him after he tried to be honest, and Satan says, "You were better off before you met God. You still had your wife then."

That's why Satan whispers in the ear of a hardworking woman, "Why do you keep praying for your son? You know God's not listening. He doesn't care for you."

And that's why he crawls under the bridge to tell a lonely young boy, "You're forgotten. You're nobody. Why don't you end it all?"

Satan specializes in lies, confusion, desperation, and depression. As a fallen angel, he is a limited being, but he still has tremendous powers and the most clever strategies. He moves in to tempt us at our particular point of need, and he always times his temptations to come when we're feeling weak, stressed, desperate, and confused. He throws his worst in our faces and then sits back to see what will happen.

When Is Something Going to Make Sense?

I had just finished speaking and singing during a huge Christian festival, and my husband, Norman, was helping me hurry across a muddy field to get to a radio interview. A tall, good-looking young man in his thirties approached and said to me, "Can I speak to you for a moment?"

I could tell by the look in the man's eyes that he was desperate. I looked at Norman, and he said, "I'll just wait for you over there." While Norman stood to one side, the man blurted, "I drove three hours today to be here and listen to what you had to say. This is my last shot. If God doesn't do something in my life today, I'm going to forget the whole thing."

It was a lovely day, with the sun shining down from a bright blue, cloudless sky. The first night of the festival had been washed out by heavy thunderstorms, and the field was practically a swamp. Suddenly, the man was down on his knees in the mud, doubled over, sobbing and saying, "They told me I had to die to everything, so I died to everything. Then they told me I had to live to everything, so I tried living to everything. When are they going to tell me something that's going to *work?*"

My interview would have to wait. I spent quite a while talking with this man about his life and about some of the things I had shared from the platform. He was trying to hold onto Christ, but the hell of perfectionism was on his back. In his frantic attempts to please God by living a perfect life, he had bought into the prosperity doctrine. In fact, he had bought into just about every new brand of doctrine that had come along. He heard that Jesus wanted him "healthy, wealthy, and wise," and he went for it with all his heart. He wound up feeling disillusioned and empty.

Then he heard that Jesus really wanted him to give up everything, to sell everything he had and give it to the poor. Or try beating himself black and blue to prove to God how much he loved Him. But all that had left him shallow and empty as well.

That day, down on his knees in the mud, this man only wanted to know when something was going to make sense. He was single, so his problem wasn't a deteriorating marriage or children out of control. He didn't have cancer or some other physical affliction, but he was very sick in his

16

soul. He felt frustrated with everything around him, with every church he had been to, with every friend he had, with his family, and most of all, with himself. He just couldn't get a handle on how to make God happy, how to please God more, or how to do enough to please Him at all.

Just before we prayed together, I looked him in the eye and said, "Don't you know that God could not love you more than He loves you right now? Even if overnight you become everything you've always dreamed of being, God will not love you any more than He loves you right now."

I'm not sure how much our hurried conversation in that muddy field helped, but when we parted, the man had a different look in his eyes. The desperation was gone, replaced by a peaceful calm resolve to know God the way God already knew him.

I hoped the man would remember some of the lines from a song I had sung that day, a song simply titled "God Loves You":

> Well, every person fails,
> And every man needs love to pick him up
> Time after time
> This world can use you up
> And leave you with a world of care
> Where hope used to shine.
> But God can give you strength
> When all you've done is fail.
> So say it till you understand.
> Tell me, do you really understand?
>
> That God loves you
> And made you for the pleasure of knowing you
> And showing you
> God loves you.[2]

From personal experience I know that holding onto heaven no matter what life throws in your face begins with understanding that God loves you and that He made you for His pleasure.

When hell is on our backs, we often ask, "Can I really trust God? Where is He? Why isn't He riding to the rescue?" Perhaps the real question is "Can God trust *me?*"

Is Jesus Worth It All?

If I say I'm willing to follow Jesus, what do I mean? I believe there is only one valid reason for following Jesus: because He is worth it. *He* is worth it—His love, His under-standing, His compassion—who *He* is. I follow Him with no strings attached, not telling God that I'll do this if He'll come through with that. Either Jesus is worth it only because He is Jesus, or *He is worth nothing*.

Those may seem like hard words to tell a teenager as he crawls into his cardboard box under the bridge to go to bed. I don't mean them as hard words, but as words of com-fort. As he struggled to survive, all Darrell Gilyard had was Jesus.

As Darrell and I talked on "Heart to Heart" that morning, I looked into the eyes of this humble, gentle, strong man and realized that he understood a principle I had struggled with for years. He asked God one question—"Why?"—and then he was willing to wait for an answer. Days turned into weeks, which turned into months and years. Darrell kept waiting for an answer to "Why?" Finally, as he prayed, the answer came. All the Lord said was "Trust me, Darrell. I have it *all* under control!"

I tried to imagine myself in Darrell's shoes, and I asked him, "Was that enough? To know that God was in control even though your circumstances never changed?"

Darrell responded by saying that he decided he had to take his eyes off his circumstances and focus them on the

Lord. Time passed, and nothing changed. Darrell still had to live with nothing. He had to go to school wearing the same shirt, day in and day out all year long, and sleep in the same cold, damp place night after night.

Although Darrell was laughed at and ridiculed, his perspective on life changed, and he experienced overwhelming peace and contentment. He survived the lonely days and nights with a song in his heart because he knew without a doubt that Jesus loved and cared for him.

Darrell finished high school and went on to earn a theology degree from Criswell Bible College. When he was twenty-two, he met and married his wife. Today they have two children, and Darrell's vision of building his own church has become a reality.

Talking with Darrell Gilyard made me thirst after God's voice because I want to hear God as Darrell heard Him—with everything under control, even the things I can't explain. If ever there was a man who held onto heaven with hell on his back, it is Darrell Gilyard. Nothing at all in his life made sense. There was no good news that he could see with his eyes, but he learned to live by faith, not by sight. He learned to live by what he knew was true because God had spoken it to his heart.

Many Questions, Few Answers

Darrell Gilyard's story is dramatic, but what was true for him is true for you and me. No matter what kind of hell may land on our backs, all we finally have is Jesus, and He is worth it because He loves us.

Yes, we still have questions. Should we hesitate to ask them because we're supposed to have all the answers? Satan loves it when we are silent, afraid to ask the questions that can lead us to understanding. In his book *True Believers Don't*

Ask Why, John Fischer wrote: "Jesus never hands truth to anyone. We must reach out and grasp it."[3]

I sometimes wonder why we aren't willing to ask more questions in a search to find the truth. Perhaps, as John Fischer suggested, we don't like questions because they "leave us vulnerable, weak, needy. They open up gaping holes in our personality, our theology, or our lifestyle. Questions force an honesty that we are unwilling to confront—an honesty that requires us to live with our lives unresolved."[4]

But living our lives with certain things unresolved is what faith is all about. I believe that many things happen that we simply can't explain. When we look back after many years, we still have little understanding of what went on, other than the knowledge and assurance that Jesus was there with us through every moment, walking by our side, guiding our footsteps. We never needed to fear the questions, because Jesus was answer enough.

Some of the greatest words Paul—or any human being—ever wrote start with questions: Can anything separate us from the love Christ has for us? Can troubles or problems or sufferings? If we have no food or clothes, if we are in danger, or even if death comes, can any of these things separate us from Christ's love?

Paul's answer is that nothing—*absolutely nothing*—in this entire world can separate us from the love of God that is in Christ Jesus our Lord.[5]

Here is where we must start. Even in the darkest night, the most blinding pain, the most maddening frustration—when nothing makes sense anymore—we hold onto heaven because He alone is worth it all. In the following chapters, I talk about choices. When our dreams go sour or seem unfulfilled, we can choose to allow Satan to slither into our lives, or we can choose to hold onto heaven, no matter how hopeless life gets. I've faced those kinds of choices myself. I want to share a little bit of how I went through my own kind of hell when the most important relationships in my life were torn from me or left hanging by a thread.

As the British writer Thomas Hardy put it, "If a way to be better there be, it lies in taking a full look at the worst." I've learned to hold onto heaven by identifying ten critical choices we all face when the worst is on our backs. In the coming chapters, we will look at each of these choices and see how people with simple, but determined, faith have been able to live in the worst kinds of situations and hold on anyway, suffering the worst kind of pain, but never letting go of the love of God in Jesus Christ.

Holding on is hard—it can seem impossible—but it is worth it because Jesus is worth it. No matter what happens, Jesus is enough.

Ten Crucial Choices We All Must Face

1. When life doesn't make sense anymore because all of hell seems to be on our backs, we can give up, or we can remember who Jesus really is and that no matter how dark it gets, *He is worth it all.*

2. When guilt, doubt, and low self-esteem occupy the secret places in our lives, we can let them cripple us, or we can allow the painful, healing light of God's love to set us free.

3. When the heat of problems and pain burns into our very souls, we can crawl away and hide when it gets too hot, or we can choose to be living sacrifices who stay on the altar for His sake.

4. Christian service is a poor substitute for Jesus Himself. We must ask ourselves, "Do I want to run myself ragged doing things for God, or do I want the best part—being His friend and knowing Him face-to-face?"

5. When promises we have made no longer seem to work or become too hard, we can choose to walk away or to stay, because we know we have made a covenant with God, and He keeps His covenants with us.

6. When this complex, plastic world tries to squeeze us into a designer mold, we can let fear and pride take over, or we can shake free to live the simple truth of the gospel with humility and love.

7. When the needy cross our path, we can choose to show selfish indifference, or we can take our eyes off our own needs and follow Jesus to love the unlovely.

8. When God seems far away and our prayers bounce off the ceiling, we can give in to despair, or we can keep holding onto heaven in simple trust.

9. When our dreams seem to go sour or remain unfulfilled, turmoil and hopelessness can dominate our lives, or we can hold onto heaven with open hands, ready to let God put in what He wishes and take out what He wills.

10. When we face our choices, large or small, we can settle for lukewarm, diluted faith, or we can seek the real thing, because we know that one life—one Christian word or deed offered with unbridled zeal—does make a difference now and through all eternity.

T W O

No Hidden Places

When guilt, doubt, and low self-esteem
occupy the secret places in our lives,
we can let them cripple us, or we can allow
the painful, healing light of God's love
to set us free.

I looked out of the airplane window as the sun sparkled on the brilliant snow. "Ladies and gentlemen, we are about to land at Denver's Stapleton Airport. Please fasten your seat belts."

I had a concert that evening in a school auditorium. We'd had a pleasant flight, and I rested for a couple of hours in our hotel room before the evening began. The concert was being promoted by a friend, and so I felt at home.

A young local girl sang before it was my turn to sing. She was good, and the crowd liked her. I could see her genuine love for Christ sparkle in her eyes, and she had a beautiful voice. As she finished, my friend walked up to the microphone: "We'll take a short break for about ten minutes, and when we come back, Sheila Walsh will be with us."

Some in the audience clapped, while others rushed to the

restrooms before the lines got too long. I shared a dressing room with the young singer, and she came bursting in.

"Wow, that was fun! Do you think I did okay?" she asked.

"I thought you were great, Sarah," I said. "The Lord really used you."

A couple of beaming faces appeared at the doorway. "Sheila," said Sarah, "this is my mom and dad."

We shook hands, and I could tell how proud they were of "their little girl." I stood by, enjoying the whole scene, but then I got my cue and told them I had to go. I almost got to the door when Sarah's father said, "Boy, your dad must be *so* proud of you."

I'm not sure why he said that. Perhaps he wanted to include me in the joy he felt about his own daughter. I know he meant what he said as a compliment, but I felt as if I had been kicked in the stomach. Without replying, I turned and pulled the door shut behind me. I didn't want them to see my face. I didn't want them to ask questions.

Your dad must be so proud of you. . . . The words brought everything back. Why, after all these years, could it still hurt so badly? Would I ever be completely free? I sat in a restroom cubicle with my head in my hands. What would it have been like if my dad had lived? Would my life have been different? Would I have been a different person? How I wanted him to be standing there that night to be proud of me, but he had been gone for a long time.

I stepped out on the stage, and I knew the only way I could get myself together was to do what I always do—be very honest with the crowd and share from my heart.

"You know," I told them, "a strange thing happened to me just a few minutes ago. . . ." I went on to talk about the incident in the dressing room. I talked about the things that hurt us, the things that wound us, and the things we don't understand.

24

I shared just a bit from my childhood—how my father had been such a wonderful Christian man who was so much fun to be with. Then one night he went to bed as warm and loving as ever, but woke up a changed man. A stroke had left him weak and confused, and for the next eleven months our family had to watch as he deteriorated before our eyes.

I didn't say much more and quickly went on with the concert, but that scene in the dressing room stayed with me. I realized that even though I had dealt with certain things in my life, the memories were still there, waiting to remind me of the pain that had invaded my childhood and changed my life forever.

The Last Good Christmas

I was born in Cumnock, a small mining town near the western coast of Scotland. Mum was a straight arrow who had loved God most of her life, never veering to the right or left. Dad's path had been a rockier one. He had served with the British Navy, and, like many young sailors, he'd "lived" a little. But when he finally gave his heart to God, he gave it all.

My dad had a very practical faith. If he saw someone with real need, he did something about it. He didn't just pray, he was prepared to be the answer to his own prayers. He was spontaneous and a lot of fun. I thought he was wonderful.

My sister, Frances, who is two years older than I, was a contented and placid child—unlike me. I was a tomboy, and when I reached my fourth birthday, I wanted a dog very badly. I wanted my own living, barking "Lassie," who would rescue me from any perilous situation, and there were many of those in my life!

One evening, when Frances and I were tucked in bed, wearing our Donald Duck pajamas, our father came into our room.

"Sheila," he said, "I want you to close your eyes and hold out your hands." I obeyed, and as I stuck out my hands, something furry ran up my sleeve. I screamed and jumped out of bed, running frantically about, trying to free myself from what felt like a rat.

"Be careful, be careful!" Mum cried. "It's a little puppy!"

I sat with eyes like saucers as Mum extracted the little dog from my pajama sleeve. It was a baby dachshund, and we decided to call her Heidi. It was just before Christmas, and my life seemed so complete. Mum had just given birth to a beautiful little boy they named Stephen. What more could we ask for!

Well, there was one other thing—a dollhouse, which I'd always wanted. It must have cost Dad quite a bit. As a traveling salesman from our farming community, he never made a lot of money, but he always provided for us.

That Christmas, however, he somehow managed to come up with the money for the dollhouse, and I thought it was the most wonderful Christmas I had ever had.

It would be the last Christmas I had with my father at home. Just a few weeks later, he went to bed one evening as my dad, a normal, healthy man, but by the next morning the father I knew was gone forever, stolen by a thrombosis in his brain that struck in the night. His power of speech was gone, and he was paralyzed down one side.

Life Changed Completely for All of Us

I don't remember very much about the next year or so. Everything was changed, nothing was sure, and life was sometimes confusing. Trapped in his stroke-crippled body, my father never spoke a word. Instead he communicated with unintelligible noises. He was able to move about with a cane, and most of the time he seemed very weak. Like most small children, I adapted quickly to my father's condition and would sit on his knee to read to him from my storybooks and tell him what I had been doing that day. I believed, "My dad still loves me. He still understands me."

But as the months went by, my father went from being warm and gentle and a hiding place for me to acting at times cold and unpredictable. He began to have "brain storms," which put him into a rage and gave him the strength of three men. Later, when he came out of them, he would realize what he had done and sit holding his head in his hands, crying like a child.

For some reason, he directed most of his anger toward me, never toward my older sister, Frances, or my baby brother, Stephen. Sometimes, he would look at me as if he hated me. I didn't know why. I was only four years old. I guessed that there had to be something horribly wrong with me; otherwise, why would my dad look at me like that?

One day, not long before I was to turn five, I sat by the fire playing with Heidi, the little puppy he had given me the Christmas before. I looked up and saw my dad coming toward me with a strange look in his eyes.

He raised his cane, and at that moment I knew that he was going to hit me. In sheer panic, I pulled the cane away from him, and he lost his balance and fell. He lay there moaning, and I was sure it was all my fault. Mum rushed in to help him, and I ran to my room and hid, trembling and afraid to come out.

Eventually, it became necessary for my dad to be admitted to a psychiatric hospital, for his well-being and for ours.

My father hung on for a few more months, and then he went "home," at peace at last with the Lord. But in my little heart, there was no peace. I would wake up in the night, crying, "Oh God, why am I so miserable? I hate myself."

Somewhere in my heart, a door slammed shut, and I buried a piece of my life for many years.

Mum Managed with a Meager Income

Left with three children under the age of seven, my Mum's prayer was "God, I pray You will spare me to see Frances and Sheila and Stephen growing up to love and trust You. That's all I ask."

With no income, Mum decided that we should move into a government-owned "Council House"—one of the homes people on a low income could rent at a reasonable rate. The government also gave Mum what was called a "widow's pension," about £16 ($28) a week, which she went down to collect every Tuesday morning. I remember distinctly that it was a Tuesday because sometimes we didn't have any toilet tissue left by Monday night!

There was never enough to pay the bills, but Mum managed somehow. She was careful with every penny, and members of the church we attended would help from time to time. Because her health wasn't the best after Dad died, Mum never went back to work. She made do with her meager pension, kept our home nice for all of us, and was always there when we came home from school.

My father's stroke, frightening brain storms, and eventual death seemed to affect me more than it did anyone else in the family. I would sit in church on Sunday and listen to the pastor say, "For those of you who have lost a husband or a dad or a mum, you can rejoice that one day you'll see them again."

But I didn't want to see my dad again. I was afraid of him.

For years after my father died, I kept having the same recurring nightmare: I saw him coming to get me because I had pushed his cane away and made him fall that day. I often woke up in the middle of the night, crying into my pillow, and I also walked in my sleep until I was sixteen. I changed from a happy, outgoing, friendly little girl to a loner who was withdrawn and introspective. I never let Mum out of my sight and was with her every possible minute.

My mum was told that I would never be "normal." I would never even want to venture outside of my home alone. I would always be afraid.

But Mum did not believe that. She would get down on her knees and pray, "God, You're bigger than this thing. And I ask that You would glorify Yourself through my daughter."

Mum was an incredible inspiration to us all. She believed God would provide what we needed, and she prayed for those needs with simple faith. She never got bitter or angry with God over her lot. She was like a rock for our family, and her faith kept us strong.

When I was eleven, an evangelist came to our town. I remember hearing him explain that God had no grand-children—only sons and daughters. Many people went forward, but I just couldn't move. That night, however, I told my mum I wanted to become a Christian. We knelt together in my bedroom, and Mum prayed with me as I became a child of God.

I Couldn't Call God "Father"

Strangely enough, however, I could not pray to God as my Father. I was still trying to bury my dad's tragedy deep inside. I blotted out that horrible night when they took my dad away, and I substituted my own fantasy: My father and I were walking along the beach and suddenly he was "taken home." There was no pain or screaming or fear—nothing like that to deal with. My dad had just gone home. I knew where he'd gone, and it was fine with me.

29

Throughout my teenage years it seemed we had an unwritten rule in our family not to talk too much about my dad because I couldn't handle it. At times I would fall into deep depression as I tried to cope alone with my bottled-up feelings. Sometimes I would sit staring straight ahead as my mother begged me to talk to her and not shut her out. Inside, I felt like screaming, but I just couldn't express my feelings. I felt as if I had fallen into a pit too deep to crawl out of, and no one could reach me.

While I coped with my inner turmoil, life went on, and much of it was good. As I entered my teens, my singing voice showed promise, and I started taking private lessons from a wonderful man named Mr. Tweddle. He was a perfectionist. After my first lesson he said, "Sheila, you sound like a cross between a sheep and a machine gun."

Mr. Tweddle assigned me to do strange exercises, like singing an incredible assortment of different phrases over and over. For a while I wasn't sure Mr. Tweddle knew what he was doing. But when he entered me in a music festival competition in which I won first place in two categories, I changed my mind in a hurry! Singing became a tremendous outlet for me. I went from being a fearful little girl who wouldn't leave my mum's side to performing in front of people—and really enjoying it!

Mr. Tweddle wanted me to train for opera, but I headed in a different direction when a gospel group called Unity invited me to join them. For two years, fifteen of us traveled all over Scotland on weekends and school holidays, singing and giving our testimonies.

One evening it was my turn to speak. I prayed for an hour before the concert, asking for the right words to say. Petrified, I talked for about fifteen minutes and, incredibly, fourteen young people became Christians that night. I was so ecstatic I couldn't sleep. That experience helped me to decide that with God it would be all or nothing. I had to tell Mr. Tweddle I could not be an opera singer, that I planned to be a missionary.

At the age of sixteen, I stood on the beach of our small fishing town and said, "Lord, everything. I'm all Yours. But I've nothing to give You. I'm an emotional wreck. I'm afraid of boys. I'm afraid of everything. I hate myself. I know I'm ugly. I hate myself, Lord. But if You could do anything with me, I'm Yours. Everything."

During the next couple of years my friends and I would go downtown at night and talk to people on the streets. Some of them were kids; some were adults who had become alcoholics; but they all had one thing in common: They had no hope. They were the kind of people my dad would help whenever he had the chance. In a way, we carried on where my dad left off.

My Mind Ran on Two Different Tracks

I didn't understand it at the time, but my mind and emotions were really running on two different tracks. Part of me was a fervent teenager who wanted to serve God, and the other part was a frightened little girl who felt guilty because she had pulled her father's cane out from under him, made him fall, and then watched as he was unable to cry for help. Had I caused my father's death? Had I made him hate me? I had never been sure, and the best way I could cope with growing up was to bottle it up inside.

When I was eighteen, I enrolled at London Bible College to study to be a missionary. I had decided that because a woman couldn't be a minister, the next best thing would be missionary work, going off into the bush somewhere and reaching the unreached with the gospel. Actually, I didn't want to be a missionary that badly. I didn't want to go far from home, but I did want God to love me always. I really loved the Lord, but at the same time I felt I had to earn His love—I never wanted Him to turn away from me.

At times, some of my friends would fall away, but I was determined that this would never happen to me. I'd tell God, "I'll never do this, Lord. I'll always hang in there. You'll always have me; I'll always love You."

As I look back, I can see that part of my motivation was really wanting to serve God, but also driving me was the fact that I just didn't like myself. I wanted to push myself harder than anybody else to prove to God that I was worthy of His love. My hidden places controlled my life, but I didn't realize it. I knew God, but I still needed a freeing touch from Him. In many ways, I was like the searching people Jesus met as He walked the dusty roads of Palestine, individuals whose hidden places kept them trapped in lives they longed to change.

We all know the story of the Samaritan woman. Sometimes we don't realize how typical she is of each of us. Surely she longed for a different life, with no hidden places, no secrets, no lying awake at night wondering where it all had gone wrong. Guilt, doubt, and low self-esteem crippled her. But she was able to free herself from their grasp.

Jesus unlocked her secret with just one statement: "Go and get your husband and come back and we can talk."

The Samaritan woman hung her head for a second as all the ugliness paraded before her eyes, and then she looked at Jesus. The time for hiding was over.

"Sir, I don't have a husband."

As Jesus looked into the very soul of this lonely, beaten woman, He saw it all—the guilt, the doubt, the low self-esteem—and He loved her. "I know," He said. "You've had five husbands, and you're not married to the man you're living with now."

There it was, out in the sunlight, revealed by Jesus' truthful, but compassionate, words. As she looked at Jesus, the woman realized that she didn't have to run anymore. He knew it all, and yet He loved her. Surely, this Man was a prophet. He had found her hidden places, her addiction to empty, meaningless relationships. All her life she had looked for someone to fill the void.

I am sure that many of us identify with that woman's story. There are few who have no hidden places. Some reach for a bottle of Scotch when the pain gets too much. Others are trapped in an endless cycle of food binges to dull the self-hatred and loneliness. And so many lash out or hide or find themselves driven because of things they suffered as a child.

Yet, we all have a choice, just as the Samaritan woman had a choice. When guilt, doubt, and low self-esteem occupy the secret places in our lives, we can let them cripple us, or we can allow the painful, healing light of God's love to set us free. The Samaritan woman believed she knew God and how to worship Him, but Jesus cut through her theology to get to the real point. Those who worship God must worship Him in spirit *and in truth.*[1]

It was then that the woman knew that she was speaking with the Messiah. She chose to "come clean," to open all the doors of her secret past and step completely into the sunlight. Satan revels in planting his seeds in the shadowy places of our lives. His bitter fruit only grows in the dark, musty places, but when the sunlight falls upon his evil crop, it withers and dies.

We never hear again of that woman. Perhaps she stood with the crowds on Golgotha hill that terrible day and watched. As the sky grew dark, she must have thought back to how it used to be, before she had met Him. She had not been the same since the light of His love had pierced her darkness. No longer could the enemy torment her with her worthlessness. She had looked in the face of God, and He was smiling.

God Finally Did a "New Thing" for Me

I had known the story of the Samaritan woman since childhood, but as I grew up I didn't realize how much we had in common. As my college years flew by, I was so busy with studies, prayer meetings, and going out with evangelistic teams that I suppose I became quite sure that I had dealt with my father's death. But the guilt and fear still lay buried deep inside. Whether praying alone or with friends, I continued the habit I had started as a young girl, seldom addressing God as Father. The only exception was when I would quote the Lord's Prayer. Then I would use the phrase "Our Father, Who art in heaven," but otherwise I always addressed my prayers to "Jesus" or "the Lord."

I never noticed this, and if someone had brought it to my attention I probably would have said I had no problem with God's being our heavenly Father. I just felt very close to Jesus, because He is our Savior and Friend.

Something else I didn't notice was how the burden I carried inside affected my relationships with the opposite sex. London Bible College was a great spot to be a girl, because there were two men to every woman, and they were all Christians. I dated a few times during my first years of school, but none of those relationships was serious. My senior year, however, was different. Dave was all I would ever want—or so I thought.

We were assigned to the same evangelistic team. He preached, and I sang. I guess I thought we would make a perfect couple, serving the Lord somewhere after we got married. But our relationship didn't last. As much as I loved Dave, something made me afraid to get totally involved with

anyone. I believed that if you gave yourself totally to someone, you gave that person the power to hurt and even break
you. What I didn't understand completely was that this phi-
losophy had come out of the terrible hurt I had experienced
with my father.

I might have gone on like this for many more years, perhaps for life, had it not been for one special day during my
senior year. Each term we had a "Quiet Day" with no lectures or regular class activities. We went to chapel in the
morning and evening, and we were free to spend the rest of
the time alone with the Lord. During morning chapel, the
speaker's text had been Isaiah 43:18–21. For some reason,
verses 18 and 19 burned into my memory:

> The Lord says, "Forget what happened
>   before.
>   Do not think about the past.
> Look at the new thing I am going to do.
> It is already happening. Don't you see it?"

After chapel I walked alone in some woods near our dorm
with my Bible and my daily study notes. I turned to the passage assigned for our "Quiet Day"—Isaiah 43:18. Throughout the day I pondered why this verse had hit me so hard.
What was I supposed to forget, and what new thing was
God doing that I didn't see yet?

I was still thinking about the verse after going back to my
room, when one of my friends came by to give me a gift. She
had copied down Isaiah 43:18 in her exquisite "copperplate"
handwriting. As I admired her lovely work, I knew that God
must be trying to tell me something. To that point, however,
I wasn't getting the message. My past was a closed book. It
had nothing to do with any new things that God might be
planning for me.

At 10:00 that night I was in the Student Common Room

watching the late news when for no apparent reason tears welled up in my eyes. I rushed back to my room, fell on my bed, and wept for over an hour. There was some kind of groaning coming out from deep inside, but I couldn't identify the cause of my grief.

Around midnight I went down the hall to talk to Jenny, who served as a student leader of our dorm. "I don't know what's happening," I told her. "There's something happening to me, and I don't know what to do. I feel as though I can hardly bear it." Jenny didn't know me very well, but she suggested that we get down on our knees and pray together. After we prayed for some time, she said, "You know, I think God is trying to tell you something about your father."

I let out a groan that was almost a roar of pain. The house where we had lived before my father's stroke and death flashed into my mind. Again I saw his confused and angry face as he came at me with that cane. I realized that something had been locked away inside. I had shut a door, and there was no way I was going to let anyone into this part of my life—not even God.

As I prayed with Jenny, I was able to face the hurt that I had refused to admit was even there. For the first time I realized that ever since becoming a Christian as a young girl I had rarely called God "Father." Now I understood why. The pain caused by my own father's death had been too much to bear, and I didn't want to link God with that.

I went back to my room and spent most of the rest of the night with a concordance and my Bible, looking up verses referring to God as Father and weeping for joy over each one.

Mum and I Needed to Talk

The next day I knew what I had to do. I went to see Mr. Kirby, our principal. I knew he would understand. Of all the people I met at London Bible College—and I thank God for every one of them—I am most thankful for Gilbert Kirby, and he is my good friend to this day. Well-read and wise, he always retains a childlike wonder at the mystery of the gospel.

I guess I looked pretty awful because I had been up all night crying, but Mr. Kirby listened carefully as I told him what had happened. Finally I said, "You know, I think I should go home. After all these years, my mum and I have never been able to really talk about my dad. I've never even had a photo of my dad. I never wanted one. But now Mum and I need to talk."

"I think it's a great idea," he said without hesitation. "I think you should do that immediately. . . . Here, let me find out when the next train leaves."

Mr. Kirby asked his secretary to call and get the train schedule. I packed a few things quickly and walked down to the station, which was only three minutes away. The four-hundred-fifty-mile trip from London to Ayr took over six hours. I spent the time reading the Bible, praying, and trying to think about what I would say to Mum—what I would ask her after all these years.

When she opened the door, her face was a mixture of surprised joy and wondering if something were seriously wrong. I said, "Hi, Mum. . . . I had to come home because . . ." Then I burst into tears. For several minutes I couldn't gather the words to tell her what had happened. All I could say was, "It's all right. . . . I'm okay. I'm okay."

She made me a cup of tea and, although she was anxious and puzzled, waited for me to gather myself together enough to tell her what had happened. I told her the whole story, especially the part about seeing our home flash before my eyes when Jenny said, "I think God is trying to tell you something about your father."

I described to Mum the picture of our home that had come into my mind, and she said, "Yes, that's what it was like. . . . That's where we lived."

And then we talked for a long time about things I had never wanted to know before, about how things had been while my father was in the psychiatric hospital in those months before he died. Mum told me everything, describing her feelings during my father's illness, the sense of emptiness when he died. She told me about the funeral and where my dad was buried. She described at length how hard it had been to commit Dad to a psychiatric hospital.

"I wonder at times if I held onto him too long," she admitted, "but it was so hard to let him go because he was my husband, and I loved him so much."

All that day and into the evening we talked, looked through photograph albums, and cried together. I stayed with Mum until Monday morning before taking the train back to school. My weekend with her had been a wonderful time of healing. The fear and guilt that had festered inside of me ever since I was five years old was finally cleansed away. I realized that what had happened to my dad was not his fault—and it certainly was not mine. I finally understood that pulling away his cane and making him fall was not an unforgivable sin, but only the act of a frightened little girl who couldn't understand what had happened to her dad.

The English poet John Donne wrote: "Look, Lord, and find both Adams met in me. As the first Adam's sweat surrounds my face, may the last Adam's blood my soul embrace." After that weekend, I could embrace the last Adam's blood with new and much deeper gratitude. Now I understood the message God had for me in Isaiah 43:18–19. I could walk away from the past and concentrate on what God was going to do with my future, because I had allowed His love to set me free.

So Many Hide Behind Their Wounds

Over the years I've learned that my story is not unique. Many people have secret places where they hide and lick their wounds. They choose to live a life of denial and doubt, rather than be honest with themselves. Sometimes they are unaware of what they're hiding, or why. But once they can face it, God does His healing work.

One of my favorite passages of Scripture comes from 2 Corinthians, where Paul spoke from personal experience: "We have troubles all around us, but we are not defeated. We do not know what to do, but we do not give up. We are persecuted, but God does not leave us. We are hurt sometimes, but we are not destroyed" (2 Cor. 4:8–9). Paul's words remind me of a wonderful song by Phil McHugh, the chorus of which says:

> In heaven's eyes, there are no losers,
> In heaven's eyes, no hopeless cause
> Just people like you with feelings like me
> Amazed by the grace that we have found in heaven's
> eyes.[2]

I enjoy and appreciate every person I interview on "Heart to Heart," but every now and then, there are people who are special. There is something about them that makes you want to wrap them up and take them home. Al Kasha is that kind of person—so warm and real. I admire him as a songwriter, too. He won an Academy Award for best song written for a movie for "The Morning After," which he wrote with Joel Hirschhorn. It became the theme for the film *The Poseidon Adventure*.

I can still remember seeing *The Poseidon Adventure* with my mum in a little Scottish theater that always showed a double feature. Somehow I got the times confused, and my mum and I had to suffer through two and a half hours of the worst John Wayne movie ever made before *The Poseidon Adventure* came on at 9:25 P.M. But we loved the film, and I rode home on the bus with Mum that night, humming, "There's got to be a morning after . . ."

It turns out that Al Kasha wrote that song out of a very personal experience. He was brought up in a poor family, living above a barbershop in Brooklyn with his brother and an incredibly cruel father. His dad was an alcoholic, who on the nights when he got very, very drunk would come home and beat Al and his brother.

He once left Al locked up in a closet and didn't remember to let him out until three days later. Al's childhood was a nightmare. In high school he got a role in the school production of *Oklahoma* and was very excited to be singing and just to be part of the whole thing. His father burst into the school theater, drunk, and caused a terrible scene. Later on, Al's father beat him badly for daring to be ashamed because of how his father had embarrassed him at the school. One day, Al had had enough. When his father tried to abuse him, Al struck back and knocked his father down and left home, never to go back.

Al's mother didn't abuse him physically, but her treatment was perhaps even more damaging. She found it hard to express her feelings. She could never tell Al, "You're doing a good job; I'm proud of you." Instead, she just pushed and pushed Al to achieve and do better and better. He isn't sure, but perhaps she felt that if she ever told him, "You know, you've really done it. I'm proud of you," she would no longer control him.

As I talked with Al on my "Heart to Heart" program, I told him I had watched the Academy Awards when "The Morning After" had been nominated. I was nervous, as I always am every year when I watch the awards ceremony.

40

My palms sweat, and I'm not even nominated for anything! Every time somebody wins, I feel as if that person is my brother or my sister, and I practically burst for joy even though I have never met them.

When "The Morning After" won and Al's name was announced, I imagined how thrilled he was when he came forward to get his Oscar. Little did I know that he was already battling the anxieties suffered by every victim of agoraphobia, fear of open places. Agoraphobics become so afraid that they want to lock themselves away in a corner and hide from the world because they just hurt too much.

Al marched up to the stage that night with Joel Hirschhorn, his cowriter. Al smiled and gave his acceptance speech, but his heart was pounding, and he was terrified that he might break down right there in front of the sophisticated Hollywood crowd.

He got through it, however, and afterward he wondered what his brother, Larry, thought. A Broadway producer, Larry had already won a Tony for *Applause*, a show starring Lauren Bacall. Al knew that Larry was his mother's favorite, although she denied it.

The next day the phone rang, and Al heard his mother's voice gushing with excitement, "L'Alfred, I'm so proud of you!"

"*Alfred*, Mom." Al couldn't help correcting her. Since Larry was always on her mind, she had a tendency to combine their names.

"An Oscar! And someday I'll bet you win a second Oscar!"

The blood drained from Al's face, and he gasped for breath. A second Oscar! The gold plating on the first was still fresh.

His mother's next statement lodged like a bullet in his brain and stayed there for the next ten years. "And someday,

41

L'Alfred darling, you'll really make it, when you win a Tony, like your brother did."[3]

Al went on to plunge into his work even further, winning another Oscar for "We May Never Love Like This Again," the theme for the film *Towering Inferno*. But it was never enough, and he fell deeper and deeper into depression. When his father died of cancer, the symptoms of his agoraphobia became overwhelming. He began to have heart palpitations and he hyperventilated when he was out in a restaurant or anywhere away from home. Soon he refused to go out to work, to appointments, anywhere.

Eventually, his wife, Ceil, could stand it no longer, and she asked him to leave. After being separated for about a month, they met to talk about reconciliation. After their meeting, Al went home, his palpitations worse than ever. He had been trying to get treatment for his agoraphobia, but in a fit of self-reproach for being weak, he had stopped going to group therapy meetings.

Al arrived home and was in such total despair that his body was trembling as tears rolled down his cheeks. Suddenly he said, "God, if You're listening, help me." He didn't feel he deserved God's love, but he ached for it. He flipped on the television set, and a fuzzy picture of the Reverend Robert Schuller flashed onto the screen. Then he heard the words, "Perfect love casts out all fear."

At first Al dismissed the words as too simplistic, but then his mind reversed them, and he found himself thinking, "Fear casts out all love." He realized that that was what had happened to him. Fear *had* cast out all love. He had been afraid to fail—his wife, his child, his partner, his parents, the artists he worked with, and his friends. He'd found it easier to imprison himself behind his phobias, hiding from the world.

Al continued to watch the Schuller broadcast. He heard

the words, "If you put your trust in Him, you'll find more peace than you've ever known." It dawned on him that his only hope was to get the focus off himself and put it somewhere else. He realized he didn't have to be perfect and take all the responsibility. He only had to be real and honest, and all God was asking from him was to do his best.

There in his room in front of the television set, Al uttered one word, *Jesus.* He kept repeating that same word, and as he did so, his fear diminished and peace started to fill his heart. He remembers, "I had a sense that a blinding light was filling the room. It seemed to me as if a window had opened. Whether the window of my soul or an actual window, I've never been quite sure. But there was an opening, a healing, a flowering inside that flooded my heart."[4]

With the television set still on, Al closed his eyes and fell asleep. The next morning he asked Jesus into his heart, and he was like a bird let out of a cage.

Later, Al reunited with his wife, and they both made public commitments to Christ at a nearby church. Slowly, he learned to conquer his fears by putting total trust in Christ. Today his anxiety attacks are gone.

Al wrote the words to "The Morning After" many years before he met Jesus, but they were to become words that fit his own life perfectly:

> There's got to be a morning after,
> If we can hold on through the night.
> We have a chance to find the sunshine;
> Let's keep on looking for the light.[5]

Al Kasha found the Light. He let it shine into his hidden places, and he's never been the same since.

Coming Out of the Dark Corners

For so many of us, it takes years to come face-to-face with the fears that lurk in our past. We bury them so deeply because we are convinced that if they were released they would overwhelm us. We don't allow ourselves to think about them even for a moment, but their long shadows cast a dark cloud over our minds nonetheless.

The Greek word for "salvation" means to save, to heal, to make complete. That is what happens at the cross. The Father is committed to shining His light into the darkest corners where fear and sorrow lurk and bring peace.

Unfortunately, you can know the joy of salvation but not always let God shine His light everywhere He would like. And where you leave hidden areas, the enemy has a home, a foothold to claw at your heart. Even after dealing with my father's death and cleaning out so many hidden places, I unknowingly kept one corner cluttered by deciding that just God and I would always be enough. I wouldn't get married. I'd just give myself to serving the Lord and reveling in my newfound relationship with my Father God.

As graduation from London Bible College approached, my resolve to stay unmarried strengthened. I knew of people who had gotten involved romantically and had become distracted from what God had called them to do. Rather than deal with the challenge of falling in love and still finding God's call, I thought it would be simpler not to get married at all.

I couched my escapism in noble terms, but I was setting myself up for real trouble in the future. I had resolved a great deal over that weekend when that verse of Scripture from Isaiah penetrated deep into my heart, but I hadn't dealt completely with the question of how to handle pain. My belief that God and I would be enough was based on an uncon-

44

scious decision never to love anyone as much as I had loved my father. If I did so, I would be too vulnerable, too open to being hurt. I wrote these words in my diary:

> When I was just a child, I learned that love can strip you bare, can take a bright and hopeful heart and in a moment tear your world apart. No warning bells or neon signs prepare you for the pain of having loved and having lost, and can we love again?

I decided that I would never love anyone enough to let him be able to inflict on me the kind of pain I felt had been inflicted on my mother. Yes, God and I would be enough.

THREE

Living Sacrifices Don't Crawl Away

When the heat of problems and pain burns into our very souls, we can crawl away and hide when it gets too hot, or we can choose to be living sacrifices who stay on the altar for His sake.

After graduating from London Bible College, I worked for several years with British Youth for Christ, as part of a team of singers, speakers, and evangelists assigned to reach young people with the gospel. I loved the work and began to catch a vision of who I was and what God could do with me if I were willing.

Then I met Norman in the spring of 1980, while I was singing at the Greenbelt Arts Festival near London. It was Sunday morning, and I was headed across a field to help lead the worship hour. I heard the sound of a car engine and wondered who could be silly enough to drive around out in the middle of the field where there weren't any roads.

A red Alfa Romeo sports car pulled up alongside, and a good-looking man with a beard and an infectious grin rolled down the window and said, "Hi, I'm Norman Miller. I'm with Word Records; you may have heard of me."

As a matter of fact, I had heard of Norman Miller. He was the head of an organization called Scope, which promoted several Christian concerts. He was famous for coming on stage in a different velvet jacket every night to introduce the appearing artists. I thought he was pretty impressive, really, but I didn't want him to know that.

"Can't say that I have," I said, smiling sweetly. "Is there something I can do for you—like giving you directions back to the road?"

"Well, I hear you have a really lovely voice. I have a great song on tape that I think you might like. Why don't I play it for you?"

"Look, I really don't have much time. I'm just going over to help lead worship. I hope it won't take too long." I got into his car, and he played the tape for me.

The song was great, but all I said was, "Well, how nice—look, I really have to get over to lead worship. Thanks for letting me hear this."

His smile was replaced by a look of disappointment, but I couldn't help that. I got out and hurried on across the field. Worship, after all, was more important than sitting in a sports car with a questionable man, and I knew that Norman Miller's reputation was definitely questionable. He was known to be a big spender who bought lots of expensive clothes and fast cars, and didn't take much of anything very seriously.

He must give God a major headache, I mused as I hurried along. *But God probably humors him and is bringing him along slowly.*

Norman Miller Popped Up Again

I completely forgot about my encounter with Norman in the field at Greenbelt, but a week later we were at another Christian convention, held at Filey, a small town some two hundred miles northeast of London. One evening after I finished singing, Norman Miller appeared again, and after telling me what a great voice I had he said, "You know, I just started a new record company, and my partner recently signed you for a single with options for an album while I was on business in the United States. I think we should have lunch."

This time I felt a bit of an obligation. I had no idea that Norman was a partner in Chapel Lane Records, with whom I signed the contract. I suppose I could at least be civil and let him take me to lunch—to talk about the record, of course.

After a long pause I said, "Okay," thinking a one-hour lunch and I'd be out of there. I didn't want to get personally involved with someone like him.

As long as I saw Norman only as a sharp, fast, "I don't need you" person, I'm sure I would have stayed miles away from him. Instead, however, when my friends learned that I was having lunch with Norman Miller, they acted as if I had made a date with the Marquis de Sade. Their comments ranged from "You've got to be joking. . . . he's not your type" to "Don't you know he's been *divorced?*"

No, I didn't know he'd been divorced, but now all the opposition had me intrigued. Two days later, when there was a break in the convention programming, Norman took me to lunch at a little Italian restaurant in a nearby fishing town called Scarborough, inspiration for the well-known song "Scarborough Fair."

After we ordered, Norman asked me what I thought was a strange question: "Did your friends disapprove when they found out you were going to have lunch with me?"

"Well, as a matter of fact, they did react. Should I be worried?"

Norman smiled, then grew serious and began to tell me his story—and he didn't leave anything out.

49

Norman Was on His Own by Fifteen

Norman was born into a Christian home and had a normal, happy life until he was eleven. Then one day when he was alone in the house with his mother, she had a heart attack and fell dead on the kitchen floor.

Norman didn't realize his mother was dead. In fact, air was still escaping from her lungs with terrible gasping sounds, and he couldn't stand it. He ran to another room, telephoned his father, and cried desperately, "You have to come home! Something terrible is wrong with Mom!"

After making the call, Norman couldn't go back into the kitchen because he was too afraid. He just stayed in his bedroom until his dad arrived and summoned a doctor. After the doctor made his examination, Norman's father came into the room and said, "Norman, your mother's gone."

Norman threw himself on the bed and screamed in disbelief and grief. He ran into the other room and asked the doctor, "If I had stayed with her I could have saved her, couldn't I?"

The doctor tried to convince Norman that his mother had been dead before she hit the floor, but Norman wouldn't listen. He kept thinking, *If I had just stayed with her, I could have done something and she'd still be alive!*

That thought haunted Norman for months and even years. Eventually his dad remarried, but life was never quite the same. When he was fifteen, Norman moved out of the house and set up on his own.

Norman married Renate, a lovely Swiss girl, when they both were very young. They were working at a Christian convention center, Norman as a young leader and Renate as a maid. She knew five languages and had decided to spend a year in England, brushing up on her English.

They say opposites attract, but in this case two similar

people came together. Norman is a perfectionist, and so was Renate. But instead of growing together they grew further and further apart. As Norman puts it, "The marriage died of boredom." Finally they separated, and, while they were living apart, Renate met another man. She ended up divorcing Norman, marrying the other man, and moving to America with her new husband and their new son.

Norman felt confused, crushed, and guilty all at the same time. It was the 1970s, and divorce was still unheard of among Christians in Britain. Norman was ostracized and was asked to leave the Christian organization where he was working at the time. A natural entrepreneur, he went into different kinds of businesses, including selling clothing and sporting goods.

Because he had a musical background and was an excellent pianist, he founded a public relations company and wound up doing promotional work for Word Records in England and other parts of Europe. He and his best friend, Ian Hamilton, built the company into a going concern, working around the clock five days a week, then partying every weekend.

Ironically enough, he was helping to promote all of the major Christian artists in England, and many from America as well, who were interested in breaking into the English market. But he was living the fast life and felt far from God.

The Man at the Pool Had the Answer

The afternoon shadows lengthened in the little Italian restaurant, but Norman and I kept talking, and he kept sharing more of his life. Until just recently, he had continued his crazy life-style, helping to build Word Records England into a bigger and better company, but always feeling empty because he knew he was walking farther and farther away from God's heart.

51

Fortunately, he had a godly secretary who said one day, "You need to read John 5."

"Okay," said Norman. "Why not?"

He read the story of the healing of the man at the pool at Bethesda, but didn't get a thing out of it. He went back to his secretary and said, "Are you sure I have the right chapter?"

"Definitely," she assured him. "You have the right chapter."

"Well, give me a clue about what all this means," he asked her.

"Norman," she admitted, "I haven't got a clue. I just know that God has something to say to you through that chapter."

Norman continued reading John 5 for several days, and then something started to make sense. The man at the pool at Bethesda had been thirty-eight when Jesus walked up one day and asked him if he wanted to be well. Norman was also in his thirty-eighth year. In a way he had been in the same state of mind as the man at the pool, who had been waiting for someone to come along to help him into the healing waters. He went back to his secretary and said, "I know what this passage means for me."

"What is it?" she asked. She wanted to know too.

"Well, I've always been waiting for a Christian girl to come along and change my life, just the way this guy was waiting for someone to help him step into the pool. Now I see that Jesus is telling me that I don't need a Christian girl to change my life. He's the one who can change me if I really want to get well."

The next day Norman went to see a pastor friend and admitted to him that his life was a mess. He told his friend about the marriage falling apart and everything he had done to show Christians he didn't need them. Then he said, "I want to get well." Norman's friend prayed with him, and Norman gave his life back to the Lord. That had been just about two months before he met me in the field at Greenbelt.

I was fascinated by Norman's honesty and openness. It was obvious to me that he was hiding nothing, and both of us were so intent that we didn't even notice the hours flying by. Finally, one of the waiters let us know we'd have to leave because they were going to be setting up for dinner patrons. As we drove back to Filey, I remember thinking that I really liked Norman Miller, and I was so glad that he had been real and honest with me.

When I returned to the office, my friends were anxious—and then angry with me. Where had I been? Why was I away so long? What did I think of Norman Miller?

"I really liked him," I told them, much to their chagrin. I was the only unmarried, female, full-time staff worker for British Youth for Christ, and they were concerned about me.

A Dozen Roses and No Card

After the Filey convention, I took a few days off and went up to Scotland to see my mum. One morning I went to the door, and there was a floral delivery man with a dozen long-stemmed red roses. But there was no card, and I honestly wondered who could have sent them. Could it possibly have been Norman? I doubted he knew where I lived.

The next day I went back down to Wolverhampton, the town in northern England where YFC made its headquarters and where many of us stayed. A couple of weeks later, the telephone rang, and it was Norman, saying that he just happened to have business in Birmingham, a few miles from me, and could we have lunch again?

The truth was, he didn't have business in Birmingham at all, but he drove the hundred and twenty miles anyway, and this time we drove over to Stratford-on-Avon to have lunch. I had told Norman that I loved Shakespeare and having lunch and visiting his birthplace made it a very special day.

That evening we went out again for dinner. Afterward as we walked to the car, he admitted that he had sent the roses, and then he added, "I don't want you to say anything to me, but I really believe that you're the person I want to marry. I don't want a response yet; I just want you to know that."

I didn't know what to say. His words staggered me, but I had to admit I really liked them. I thought it was all very romantic. When I went back to my quarters at Youth for Christ, where I lived with my other friends, I didn't tell them I had had another date with Norman because I knew they'd be upset.

About a week later, he telephoned and invited me to spend the day with him in Wales. He knew of an inn near the village of Llandrindod Wells where we could have lunch and spend some time talking.

I told my roommate where I was going. She must have mentioned it to somebody in YFC, because on Monday morning I was called into the main office and advised to stop seeing Norman Miller. I was outraged by what I felt was an incredibly unjust attitude, and I said so.

"How dare you not forgive somebody whom Jesus has forgiven? Every one of you here is married—you have nice homes and families, a place to go home to. You don't care that Norman's been divorced for eight years and that his wife has remarried and has a son by another man and is living in America. You don't care that he goes home to a cold house every night, closes the door, and looks at four walls. You'd rather he live that way until the day he dies and be miserable than to have him find happiness again."

I Needed Time to Think

I was so angry I didn't even wait for a reply. I stomped out of the room and slammed the door. The days and weeks that followed were tense and confusing. I needed to get away and think. I went to my bank and withdrew every penny I had. Later that day, I went into a travel agency and asked for rates on a trip that would take me as far away as possible.

"How about North Africa," the agent said. I said, "Great!"

I paid for my entire trip then and there—my round-trip ticket to Tunisia as well as the cost of staying in an obscure hotel in Hammamet, a tiny village on the northeastern coast. I knew it was crazy, but I had to get away and be by myself. For all I knew, I wouldn't have a job when I got back, and I would be broke as well.

But I didn't care. I had to know whether Norman and I were right. He had messed up a large part of his life. He had been very wounded by it, and so had other people. Now he had found his way back to God, and if I was not the woman for him, I wanted to know that. I didn't want to interfere with what God was doing in his life.

When Norman heard the news, he didn't want me to go. "Why would you do *that?*" he asked incredulously.

"I need to get away from everybody. I need to get away from you . . . from my friends . . . and from the people I work with. I'm tired of having people tell me what God's will for my life is. I've got to get away and think this through."

Norman wasn't keen about my flying off to North Africa alone, but he understood my need to get away. When I called my mum the night before I left to tell her what I was doing, she nearly had a fit. When I said, "I'm going away for a few days," she thought I meant to some place in Britain on YFC business. When I said North Africa, all she could see was her little girl being abducted and sold into white slavery. I told her I'd be fine and that I'd see her in two weeks. I left the next morning.

When I arrived at the hotel in Tunisia, I learned it was the off-season and the place was practically deserted. That was fine with me. I spent most of my time walking and talking with God, up and down the shores of the Mediterranean Sea, which was only a few feet away from my door.

I wasn't looking for jagged lightning bolts in the sky or a yes on my pillow, written in blood. I simply wanted to find a place of peace where I could think and ask God to give me no peace if Norman and I weren't right for each other.

Soon it was time to leave and, while I had no break-through revelation, I did find the peace I was looking for. Norman met me at Heathrow Airport, and as we drove back to London in the pouring rain, I told him I believed it was right—that we should be married. In a way, that ride in from the airport completed one of the longest proposals in history. Over four months before, Norman had said, "I think you're the woman I should marry," and now I was saying, "Yes, I will marry you."

I Was Ready to Leave YFC, Regardless

The next morning Norman and I went together to see my superiors at the YFC office. I told them, "You know, I've spent a lot of time thinking and praying about this, and I want you to know I'm going to marry Norman. You've already told me that you'd ask me to leave if I went ahead with this, so I'm happy to accept that. I know you're doing this because you care about me, but I've got to hear God's voice for myself."

Instead of dismissing me on the spot, they seemed more understanding and willing to talk about it. They really seemed to care, but I felt I should leave anyway, as soon as it could be worked out. It would be no start for Norman and me if I were working for an organization that basically disap-proved of our relationship and felt that our marriage would never make it. We all decided that I would continue working until a month before our marriage, and then I would leave YFC quietly with no commotion.

That night, Norman and I had dinner. As we talked, he began to say things like "Look, I don't think I'm very good news for you." It sounded to me as if he were trying to back out because I had a nice, neatly organized life and everybody liked me. "Since so many people are against our marriage," he said, "perhaps it would be better if I just got out of the picture."

Of course, that made me all the more determined not to let go because I knew Norman was a special person and the man God wanted me to marry.

Because I still had several months to go on my yearly commitment to Youth for Christ, I decided to take each day as it came. Norman and I planned to get married in July, even though we weren't officially engaged. He changed all that in March.

I was singing at a Youth for Christ convention in the north of Wales in a town called Prestatten. Over eight thousand young people were there and, as usual, it was rainy spring weather. Everyone had to stay in little chalets that were damp and musty. Norman came up for the weekend, stopping on the way at a Welsh town to find a lovely old diamond engagement ring in an antique store. He also stopped to pick up one red rose.

As crowded as the town was, somehow I ended up with my own private chalet. When Norman came in that night he gave me the rose. Then he got down on his knees on the damp floor, put the ring on my finger, and looked into my eyes and asked, "Will you marry me?"

He had no idea of my ring size, but it was a perfect fit! It was absolutely beautiful, and I thought the whole thing couldn't have been more romantic.

Norman had to leave that same night to get back to London on business, and I ran out to tell somebody what had happened. I wanted to show somebody my lovely new engagement ring. The first person I bumped into was my YFC colleague, one of my closest friends, who said, "Oh, Sheila . . . how are you doing?"

"Hi!" I practically bubbled. "I just wanted to show you!" I held up my hand. She took one look at the ring and shook her head and walked away with tears rolling down her cheeks.

My friend's reaction set the tone for the rest of that week—sad and bittersweet. A few of the kids who were there for training hugged me and told me how happy they were for me, but all the people who knew me, all the people I felt should trust me, the people with whom I had worked for years, just looked at me strangely. I felt angry, sorry for myself, and cheated. I remembered how much fun it was when my sister had become engaged. I wouldn't have an engagement party because, obviously, I thought no one would want to come.

We became engaged on a Friday night, and I had another week to go before the convention would be over. It was a long week, and whenever I walked into a staff prayer meeting or into the staff dining room, I felt as if people stopped talking and looked away. The silence was so pregnant I could hear the clink as I picked up my coffee cup. When the coffee ran out of the urn into the cup, the gurgle sounded like a waterfall.

To my face, people were kind, but I knew what they were thinking and saying behind my back. My keyboard player was more honest than most. He told me that people were giving our marriage three years before they'd have to help me pick up the pieces.

The Wedding Included Eighteen Guests

Mercifully, the convention finally ended. I went back to Wolverhampton, where I wrapped up my commitments to British Youth for Christ. I left BYFC at the end of May and went back home to Scotland to prepare for the wedding, which would be in July. It would be in our Baptist church in Ayr, and only our families would come. I knew that none of my YFC friends would want to attend, so I decided to keep it small, strictly family members or people so close I had called them "uncle" and "aunt" while growing up. I think the total number of people invited was eighteen.

My preparations for the wedding were as bittersweet as my engagement announcement had been. My sister had had a big elaborate wedding, with two hundred guests and a band. She wore a beautiful gown with layers and layers of dreamy fabric, and she had three bridesmaids.

Because nothing about our wedding seemed to fit into *Bride Beautiful,* I decided to keep things very simple. With all the antagonism and bitterness among so many of my Christian friends, why go into debt for a big fancy affair? So I took all the money I had—about 150 pounds (or $225)—went down to a store, and bought a very simple dress. It was about as simple as a bridal gown could be.

As I got dressed for the wedding on that morning of July 21, I didn't have a shadow of a doubt that we were doing the right thing. Nonetheless, it was difficult for me when I stood at the door of the church with my brother, Stephen. There stood Norman at the front of the church, and there I stood at the back, suddenly overwhelmed with sadness because my father wasn't there to give me away.

Stephen's lip was trembling. He was having a hard time because he had never done anything like this before. I'm sure both of us were thinking about our dad and how wonderful it would have been if he had been there that day. But Stephen was there for me, and I was so proud of my tall, handsome brother, who had been a friend to me all my life.

Edwin Gunn, our pastor, conducted the ceremony. Before the wedding he counseled with Norman and me several times. He knew the whole story—that Norman's first wife had a child by another man and was now in America, remarried with still another child. He felt that door had closed and that we could marry, but he did say to Norman, "Would you feel comfortable acknowledging to the people present that you have taken these vows before and failed to keep them?"

"Yes, I'd really like to do that," Norman said, and so we planned a special "time of repentance" before we took our vows. Edwin, who had been my pastor since I was a teenager and was a good friend, did a beautiful job of communicating Norman's regret and repentance of what had happened in his prior marriage and his commitment to making our marriage work.

I Held Back a Tiny Part of My Heart

As I took my vows that day, I was sure I meant them with all my heart. What I didn't understand was that I still had unfinished business that had begun with my father's death when I was a young girl. Yes, I'd come to terms with a lot of things and realized that I wasn't to blame, but unconsciously I had resolved never to love anybody that much again. To do so would mean making myself too vulnerable. Deep within, I feared that if I loved Norman as totally as I had loved my dad, he could be taken from me, just as my father had been taken, and that would have been unbearable.

After the ceremony, we had a dinner for everyone at a local hotel, where we were served a lovely meal. Everyone was very loving and supportive and wished Norman and me the best in our new marriage.

Afterward, they all came out to wave good-bye as we drove out of the parking lot in Norman's new Rover, which had replaced the Alfa Romeo. We headed south to Keswick, a popular holiday spot in England's northern lake country, where we planned to honeymoon.

As we crossed the border from Scotland into Cumbria, a thunderstorm blew up. We both grew very quiet as Norman drove carefully through the blinding rain. Suddenly, all the pressure was off. Nobody cared anymore whether we got married or not because we'd gone ahead and done it. Then the horrible feeling struck me: *I hope we didn't do this just to spite everybody.*

I wondered why Norman was so quiet. Was he thinking what I was thinking? I was afraid to ask, and so I sat there in silence.

We had rain, thunder, and lightning for the rest of the trip, and I don't think we talked the entire time. We got to the hotel at Keswick, and Norman asked if I was hungry. I said I wasn't sure, so he had the proprietor send up some sandwiches and tea to our room. We ate very little and went to bed. We were both so tired that we were asleep in minutes, not exactly the stuff that movies are made of!

The next morning we got dressed, had breakfast, and strolled into town. I suddenly realized that everybody was looking at me. Every second person seemed to come up and say, "Hello, Sheila. . . . Hi, Sheila, good to see you." Suddenly it dawned on both of us. The biggest annual Christian convention held in Britain each year is at Keswick, and our honeymoon had fallen on exactly the same date! It seemed that every Christian in England was in town, and most of them seemed to know me.

"Norman, we've got to get out of here, fast," I said in desperation, "or we'll never be alone!" He agreed, so we went back to the hotel, packed our bags, and headed south. It was still raining, and about fifty miles north of London we were involved in a six-car pile-up. A car pulling a trailer had suddenly jackknifed and spun around, hitting the car directly in front of us. We smashed into it, banging our heads on the windshield. Then cars behind us banged into our car, turning it into total junk.

I thought the people in the car ahead of us might be dead, and I could hear one woman screaming. As I got out of our car, I could see a man whose arm was pinned in his car. It was chaos. We were fortunate that our injuries weren't more serious.

I heard Norman say, "Look, why don't you sit over here by the side of the freeway and wait for the police?" Then he went off to see what he could do to help. I remember sitting on the ground in the pouring rain, thinking, *This is what the rest of my life is going to be like.* My romantic expectations had run smack into life's realities. *Why had I done this? Why hadn't I listened to my friends at YFC? Had they been right?*

Two hours, many police, and several ambulances later, we ended up with our Rover on the back of a tow truck. We rode in the cab all the way to the south of England, where I was booked to sing at a Christian youth camp. As the tow truck driver blew smoke in our faces for the entire journey, I kept thinking, *Big jolly honeymoon this . . . no stinking engagement party . . . horrible wedding dress . . . and here I am in a tow truck, coming back from my honeymoon smelling like an ashtray.*

Our Totaled Car Was a Symbol

So we started married life with our car getting totaled. In a way, it was a symbol of what was to follow. I tried to fit into my new role as wife and homemaker while Norman worked in his office, which was located in our dining room. Every day his secretary came in, and he spent the day dictating letters involved with his new business, Chapel Lane Records. He had left Word Records England more than a year before to start the new business with a friend. Chapel Lane's studios were located in Hereford, about one hundred miles away, and Norman was in constant communication with his partner by mail or on the telephone.

Norman's place was already lovely, beautifully kept, and almost perfect, but I wanted to give it my own special touch. I began by cleaning out some drawers, and while doing so I came across a pack of old photos. There was Norman on another wedding day. Ever since I'd known him, he'd had a beard, but in these pictures he was clean shaven and looked much younger, bright-eyed and happy. There was a pretty girl beside him—and she wasn't me.

I wondered whether I should show Norman the old photos of him and Renate, then decided, why not?

That night as he was working late in the dining room/ office, I said in what I hoped was a lighthearted tone, "I found these pictures today."

I showed them to him, and he said, "I thought I'd destroyed all of these." Then he took them, threw them in the garbage, and kept right on working. Obviously, he didn't want to talk about it.

As I lay in bed that night, I thought, *I wonder what it was like for them? I bet when they got engaged, it was different. I bet it was happy and light and youthful, and they were looking forward to the whole of life together. I wonder what went wrong? I wonder when it went wrong? I wonder how long it took before it went wrong?*

For the first few weeks I got along fairly well because I did all the things a new bride was supposed to do. Mum and my grandmother had taught me how to cook, and every night I'd try out a new recipe. But just as we were sitting down to eat, the phone would ring. Norman would say, "This will just take a minute," and then he would get into a conversation that usually lasted for thirty minutes to an hour.

The calls almost always came from Norman's partner, Rob, or Rob's wife, Marian. That first year of our marriage, Chapel Lane Records was in serious financial trouble with all sorts of problems. Norman would be on the phone with both of them, trying to give comfort, advice, and reassurance.

I'd often sit there thinking, *Great. Marian's on the phone crying, and you're comforting her. I'm here after cooking this jolly meal, and it's the fifth time this week that it's gone into the garbage. We've got the best fed garbage can in England. How about comforting me? I'm the one you married.*

When I complained to Norman, he would get cross and say, "Look, I'm trying to pull this together for you as well as for me. This is our future. There is no point in getting upset about meals getting cold. I have to do this!"

After a few months, I decided I would pull back a little— just enough for some protection. I'd gone into the marriage with everything I had, but I quickly realized it wasn't the life I had hoped for. Trying to make Norman and the marriage live up to my expectations kept me on the raw edge all the time. I thought, *I can't live like this. This hurts too much. I'll develop other interests. I'll have friends. I'll depend on myself. I'll make my own life.*

I Needed "Footwashing for Beginners"

My decision to back off and make my own life was my first major mistake in my marriage. Because I didn't know how to communicate my frustration to Norman, and because he didn't seem to want to listen anyway, I began to isolate myself from him in subtle ways. As a new bride, I knew little of trying to be a servant to my mate. I thought he was supposed to cherish and serve me! Now, years later, I can see that every church should offer a course on "footwashing for beginners." From the moment we come into the kingdom of God, we need to be helped to understand a basic principle laid down by Jesus Himself: "If one of you wants to become first, then he must serve the rest of you like a slave" (Matt. 20:26).

So many passages of Scripture are very familiar to us, and yet I wonder how much time we take to really meditate on the implications of these words for our lives on a daily basis. Sometimes, for example, I like to imagine what the scene must have been like the evening of the Last Supper when Jesus gave His greatest lesson on servanthood.

Before sitting down to a meal together, it was Jewish practice to be sure that everyone's feet had been washed. Open sandals were standard footwear, and all the roads of Palestine were dry and dusty. Those same roads, by the way, were shared by animals whose masters were seldom concerned about where they left their waste. To maintain Jewish standards of cleanliness, it was necessary that everyone's feet be washed before sitting down to eat a meal.

In most Jewish homes, a servant would be at the door with a pitcher and a towel, ready to get down on his or her knees to wash the feet of guests as they arrived. But on the night of the Last Supper, there was no servant. There were only Jesus and His twelve followers.

Picture the scene: The first disciple arrived, looked into the room, and saw that no one was there doing any footwashing. "Typical," he said to himself. "They haven't gotten anyone to handle it. Well, I'm certainly not going to do it."

And so that disciple reclined at the table, his feet unwashed. Then two more disciples arrived, and seeing one disciple already at the table, thought to themselves, "Well, if he's not going to do it, I don't see why we should do it."

And so they reclined also, followed by the rest of the disciples, until they were all gathered around the table—twelve grown men with dirty feet!

When Jesus arrived, He, of course, didn't have thoughts of "Well, this certainly isn't for Me; after all, *I'm* their leader." Instead, Jesus saw the opportunity to teach His disciples one of their most important lessons.

The meal was barely underway when Jesus, the King of kings and Lord of lords, knowing what lay ahead—the spiritual, emotional, and physical turmoil that would tear His soul apart—stood up and took off his outer clothing. John, in his Gospel, described what happened next:

> Taking a towel, he wrapped it around his waist. Then he poured water into a bowl and began to wash the followers' feet. He dried them with the towel that was wrapped around him. (John 13:4–5)

He got all the way to Peter before there was any protest. "Oh, no, no, no, Lord!" Peter objected. "You don't need to do this. No, please sit down. One of us should have been doing it in the first place."

But by then it was too late, because Jesus had looked right into their hearts and could see them as they really were—and as we all are.

Our Sense of Right Is Built In

There is something built into every human being that says, "I have rights!" When we read in Romans 12:1 that all Christians are "living sacrifices," it sounds so noble. We hold onto that wonderful thought without ever wondering what the implications might be. When Paul used the words *living sacrifices*, he meant something much different from the old system.

In the Old Testament, a lamb was not consulted as to how it felt about being offered as a sacrifice. It was simply slaughtered and laid on the altar to be consumed by the fire. But in the New Testament—the New Covenant—we are living sacrifices. The trouble is, a living sacrifice can crawl off the altar when it gets too hot. God could have pre-programmed us as robots who serve Him without choice, but instead He has given us the ability to choose.

The more I walk with the Lord, the more I understand that every day of my life, for the rest of my walk on this earth, I can choose to stay on the altar, or I can choose to crawl away. When the heat is turned up, I can crawl off and say, "Well, this is not what I signed up for. I thought that this would make me feel good. I thought that all my prayers would be answered, but it seems as if God has turned a deaf ear to my cry."

But there is another choice. When the heat turns up, I can determine to be a sweet-smelling sacrifice to God, just as Jesus did.[1] As the prophet Samuel said, "To obey is better than sacrifice, and to heed is better than the fat of rams."

When Jesus washed His disciples' feet, He set the perfect example of obedience for all of us. John must have remembered that night as he wrote one of his Epistles and said, "Whoever says that God lives in him must live as Jesus lived" (1 John 2:6).

When I got married, I thought I knew all about the footwashing scene in John's Gospel. The truth is, I had much to learn about what it really means for my life. Instead of living as Jesus lived, I quietly decided to live as I wanted to live, but, of course, I would still try to be a very respectable and obedient Christian. After all, I was simply trying to protect myself from being hurt. *Who could really blame me for that?* I thought.

Traveling Separate Ways Didn't Work

We were attending a Baptist church at the time, where there were really nice people who cared a great deal for us. But I didn't feel close enough to anyone to share my disillusionment as a new bride, and I felt too ashamed to ask for help.

After we had been married about six months, I started doing tours with my first album done for Chapel Lane Records, *Future Eyes*. Norman arranged to have *Future Eyes* released with Sparrow Records in the United States, and that involved several trips to the States. Our schedule soon found me going off on tours to places like Norway, while Norman had to travel to the States on business.

After a month or two of this routine, Norman said, "This isn't going to work. You're either going to have to stop doing what you do and be home, or I'm going to have to stop doing what I do. Somehow we've got to figure out how to work together." Despite the tension and my disappointment—which I was keeping well bottled up—we still missed each other.

Our problem was solved in part when Billy Ray Hearn, head of Sparrow Records and a good friend of Norman's, called and said, "I'd love Sheila to come over and tour the States. We have an artist named Phil Keaggy, and Sheila can open for him."

So it was arranged that we would do sixty different cities with Phil, from coast to coast.

I was excited and pleased with the tour idea. It was going to be great because I knew Americans loved Scottish people. And, of course, I never doubted that they'd love me and understand that I was a nice person. I soon learned that Americans are like anyone else—you win some and lose some.

We opened our tour in Houston, Texas. I went on stage

wearing a jumpsuit with my hair short and kind of spiky, because that's how people were wearing their hair then in London. The theater was filled with Christians, but halfway through my first song, people started getting up to leave.

Where are they all going? I wondered. *They can't all need to go to the restroom at the same time.*

I finished "Love in My Life," the first song on my *Future Eyes* album, but as I continued through the concert, other people left as well. We used a lot of smoke and bright lights, and I thought we had a great time. But I learned afterward that many in the audience were just horrified at this bizarre "punk rocker" from England, and they hadn't liked me one little bit. A lot of Phil Keaggy's audience was on the conservative side, and they'd come to see someone like Phil. I was not what they had expected.

As the tour progressed across the South, I heard that some people were having loud prayer meetings, beseeching God to deliver me from my worldliness.

There were bright spots, though. We had a wonderful time in Florida, and the West Coast people were also great. We traveled in a big Winnebago recreational van—nine of us in all—covering massive distances between concerts. I just couldn't get over the size of the United States. On our trip from Dallas to Los Angeles, we drove a day, a night, and part of another day. From anywhere in the United Kingdom, if you drove for more than eight hours, you'd fall off the top!

Despite my mixed reception, the tour was successful. I also promoted my first single, "Mystery," which eventually went to number one on the Christian charts in the United States. We covered sixty cities in four months, and then headed back to England to rest and regroup.

I Settled for a "Friendly" Relationship

In some ways, Norman and I got along better on the tour than we did at home, because I accepted the fact that when we were on the road we didn't have a lot of time to spend together. We settled into a routine of getting to the next town, giving the next performance, grabbing a few hours' sleep, and then moving on.

I'd almost come to the point of thinking of Norman and myself as good friends. I had lowered my expectations about marriage, and we developed a relationship that was fairly cordial and easygoing. It wasn't what I thought marriage was supposed to be like, but I thought it was okay at the time.

In 1983, we lined up another tour of the United States to coincide with the release of my next project, *War of Love*. Again, Norman scheduled sixty cities, and we brought along our own band from England.

We started off, and things went well for a while. Norman became worried and withdrawn, but he wouldn't share the real problem with me. A little more time between concerts seemed to be available on this tour, possibly because our bus covered ground faster than the old Winnebago had before. I'd ask Norman if he could spend some time with me—maybe just a day or a half day off. "Can we just go out to dinner together?" I would plead. "Can we go and do *anything* together today?"

"Look, I've got to get on with this," Norman would say in a tired voice. "I've got to work on the books. Things are in a mess."

During the rest of that tour, our uneasy friendship truce began to unravel because I was starting to get really angry with Norman.

When the tour ended, the sound company had not been

paid, nor had the lighting company. Even the band hadn't been paid, and Norman remained responsible. We flew back to London, after playing to big crowds and selling a lot of records, but in the biggest financial hole of our lives.

Norman wouldn't even consider filing bankruptcy. He stuck to his commitments.

In order to pay our debts, Norman had to sell our home. The proceeds covered just about everything. We were left with no money, wondering where we were going to live.

We Wound Up Living with Strangers

Several months before our tour, Norman had done a concert with a man named Gerald Coates, pastor of a house fellowship in south London. Just after losing our house, we had dinner with Gerald and his wife, Anona. After hearing of our troubles, they invited us to live with them for a few months until we got on our feet.

Norman thought it was a great solution, but I thought it would be awful. I didn't even know this man. And now I would have to share a kitchen with his wife and three boys!

We moved in anyway, because we really didn't have much choice. I tried to go along with it and be very supportive. I had heard that in this kind of church people were very loving to one another.

Gerald's house fellowship had begun with a few people meeting in Gerald's home. Just recently they had grown to the point where they had to meet in a school hall. Because these people knew I was a gospel singer, I did my best to keep up a façade of everything's being fine in our marriage. In private, however, I would say to Norman, "Look, I think we need to get help."

"Well, what do you mean, what's wrong?"

71

"I'm not happy," I said.

"Well, why aren't you happy?"

"Norman, I don't think we ever talk to each other."

"Okay . . . talk to me," he said.

"No, I don't mean that way. . . ."

"Well, I don't know what you're going on about. When you decide on what you want to talk about, I'll be downstairs in the study."

I began to wonder, *What's the point? If Norman can't see my problem, maybe it's all me. Maybe I'm just a neurotic wife making unreasonable demands.*

So once again I retreated back into my shell and tried to make the best of it. The "few months" with Gerald and Anona Coates became a few years, and they became dear friends. I went back out on the concert circuit and performed tours all over England and Europe. Norman had given up his share of Chapel Lane Records in return for exclusive rights to my albums and any future albums I would produce.

We became very busy doing concerts, traveling, and selling records in all kinds of evangelical settings all over England as well as France, Belgium, Switzerland, and Spain. Norman was not only my manager, but he also traveled with me as director of all my tours.

As we got busier, I began to wonder whether Norman would ever talk to me as my husband, instead of always seeming to relate to me as my manager. I felt that as my husband he should have known that I would become exhausted. Yet, he kept asking me to do one more interview, cover one more concert date. I began to grow more and more irritated, and while I'd moan and complain a little, I couldn't admit to anyone how I really felt.

One day we got a call from two of my old Youth for Christ colleagues. They both wanted to apologize for the way things had been before our marriage. The wife was sorry that she hadn't been there as my friend when she had disagreed with me. And they both asked Norman to forgive them for judging him as well.

Norman was great about it. He was always very forgiving and would never bear a grudge. I was so glad to reconcile with them because I had missed their friendship. At the same time, however, the irony of it all left a bitter taste in my mouth. They were apologizing for how they had acted, but I had already begun to wonder whether they had been right.

But they'd never hear it from me. I'd live with it if it killed me. I'd never leave my marriage.

So I went along, simmering like a teakettle, but never really boiling over. As I look back, I realize that I was a coward. I was afraid to confront the situation head on and accept the consequences. I thought I couldn't deal with the emotional stress. I was afraid things would just get out of control, and I didn't want a lot of anger and pain because that reminded me too much of what had happened with my father. I had dealt with the guilt I felt over my father, but not with the rest of my problems.

The altar was getting hot, and I was sorely tempted to start crawling off. For now I chose to honor my covenant with Norman and God, but that commitment would falter, as you'll see in later chapters. We might choose to stay on the altar at one time in our lives, but Satan doesn't end his battle there. He continues to jab at us, hoping that we will falter as the fire gets hotter and hotter. I have yet to meet a Christian who hasn't discovered that the altar can get too hot at times. One reason I love to do "Heart to Heart" is that I keep meeting people who know what staying on the altar is all about.

The Altar Never Cools for Joni

Mention Joni Eareckson Tada's name to believers in almost any country of the world, and smiles will break out everywhere. We all love her so much and know her story so well: a beautiful and promising young athlete whose spinal column was severed in a diving accident.

We've probably all seen Joni's movie and read her books. We know that at one time she wished she could die because she couldn't deal with being handicapped. She even tried to persuade her friends to give her enough pills to end it all.

We marveled with Joni at the prospect of not being able to blow our own noses, comb our own hair, or reach out and touch someone. And through it all, Joni has become our hero.

In Pat Robertson's dressing room at the "700 Club" hangs a beautiful picture drawn by Joni, a verse of Scripture that she has illustrated. She's a gifted artist, a wonderful writer, and a beautiful singer. For many of us, the book is closed. She had a terrible accident; she struggled with her faith; she triumphed; and now she is living happily ever after.

Not so. When I spent time with Joni recently, I realized that her story lives on every single day. It takes her almost two hours to get ready every morning. For twenty years now, she has lived in a wheelchair, unable to do anything for herself.

Joni is very honest and very candid; she also has a great sense of humor. But along with all that, she has the desires of any woman. In the evening when her husband comes home after a busy day of teaching high school, she longs to be able to get up and throw her arms around his neck and say, "Welcome home! What kind of day have you had?"

Joni longs to be able to set a candlelit table, to do all the little things that we love to be able to do for each other, but she'll never be able to do them.

We Always Hope the Lord Will Hurry Up

We Christians say that we are willing to learn lessons from God, but our attitude really says, "Hurry up, Lord, and get on with it. I need to get this over with. If You have to teach me something that will help me to be a better Christian, okay. But if you could do it before lunchtime, I'd be very grateful, because I really do have a hectic schedule."

During the long days, weeks, months, and years of being immobile following her accident, Joni had plenty of time for the Lord's lessons. She learned to live day in and day out, year after year with the reality of a broken body. Even though she was paralyzed, in her heart Joni could have crawled off the altar as quickly as anyone had she chosen to do so.

Joni could have given up on God. She could have raged at Him for the rest of her life, for allowing that horrific accident to happen. She could have listened to Satan's subtle promptings to feel sorry for herself. Instead, she chose to be a living sacrifice, and she continues to make that choice daily. Every time she wakes up, her body reminds her that it's another day that she has to make a choice—one more day to love God; one more day to trust Him.

It would be so much easier if life were like a game of riddles in which God gives us hints about the right questions to ask. Then we could solve our riddles and move on. But life is not a game. It's really a worship service, and each of us is a living sacrifice.

Every time I think of Joni Eareckson Tada, it strengthens my resolve to stay on the altar for the right reasons.

But back in those early years of marriage, I stayed on the altar for other reasons—pride, stubbornness, and mostly fear. I vowed never to quit, but it only got harder and harder.

Occasionally, I would ripple the waters just a bit. Then Norman would start to become irritated with my complaints, so I would just back off. I kept telling myself, *Keep the lid on, Sheila. It's the only way you'll be able to deal with this.*

That decision lasted for quite a few years, during which time my struggle to hold onto heaven with hell on my back shifted to another area of my life: my career and the threat of losing one of my most treasured possessions.

F O U R

Be God's Friend, Not Just His Servant

*Christian service is a poor substitute
for Jesus Himself. We must ask ourselves,
"Do I want to run myself ragged doing things for God,
or do I want the best part—being His friend
and knowing Him face to face?"*

"I'm sorry, Sheila, but you're going to have to forget this concert tour. You have a growth on your left vocal cord. You not only shouldn't be singing, but you shouldn't even talk for a while."

London's leading throat specialist started putting away his instruments while I sat there—stunned. The pain in my throat had started about ten days before. I had gone to my regular doctor, who gave me some antibiotics that he said would take care of the problem. But they hadn't taken care of the problem; in fact, my throat had become much worse.

Next I had prayed with leaders in our church for healing. While I had never been the type who needed a miracle a day before breakfast, I did believe 100 percent that I would be healed. This particular tour was just too important for me to let Satan win. In fact, after the prayer session, I went out into our garden and marched up and down, thanking God for everything He had ever done, including my healing. But afterward, I sounded more like a hoarse cat than ever.

With the tour due to start in just a couple of days, I made an appointment with the top throat specialist in London, hoping that he could give me a wonder pill or maybe a shot that would somehow make it possible for me to sing. Now I sat there in shock and disbelief. I had come for a saving reprieve, not a sentence of doom. Didn't the doctor understand that 25,000 tickets had already been sold for the biggest Christian concert tour in Britain's history?

"How long must I go without singing or even talking?" I asked. "Are you absolutely sure I can't do the tour?"

"Absolutely!" he said with the clipped firmness that specialists seem to favor. "You are not to sing or even speak for at least thirty days. Then, we'll see. I may as well tell you that it's possible I'll have to operate, and you may never sing again."

How Could This Tour Be Off?

I remember leaving the doctor's office and stepping onto a busy London sidewalk on one of those unusually bright sunny days that occasionally happen in May. The brilliant sunshine seemed to mock my somber mood. Somber? It was closer to total despair. How could I tell Norman that the tour was off? He had spent innumerable hours putting it all together, and we were so sure that God's hand was on every step.

After losses and debts from our second American tour forced us to sell our home and move in with friends, I became the host of the "Rock Gospel Show," a thirty-minute program that aired once a week to about four million viewers. Because of BBC policy, I couldn't say a lot about my personal faith, but even playing Christian songs and making brief comments had people writing in to ask for more about the God I was talking about. Who was this Jesus? How could they know Him?

Norman and I had talked about how we could reach these people, and then the idea came to us: a mega gospel tour of all Britain, in the biggest theaters in every good-sized community. The whole thing had gone beautifully—until now. Most of the theaters were sold out, but it would all have to be canceled. I took the train back to the suburbs, and Norman met me at the station. "Did he give you something?" was his immediate question. "Did he give you a spray or something for the pain?"

Following doctor's orders, I started writing something on a piece of paper. He had told me, "The minute you leave this room, I don't want you to say a thing. Use this pad and pencil from now on.'"

So my first note to Norman said, "You have to cancel the tour."

Norman looked at me in total disbelief. "What do you mean I have to cancel the tour?"

I saw that I could never write fast enough to answer all Norman's questions, so I decided I would break the doctor's rule just this once.

"Okay, I'm going to talk to you now, but this will be it. The doctor told me I have a growth on my vocal cords, and I can't speak for a month, never mind singing. I might have to have an operation, and it's even possible I'll never be able to sing again. I can't say anymore to you now. You just need to know that you have to cancel the tour, and I'm so sorry."

When we arrived home, it seemed as if a black cloud had moved in from the sea and descended upon our heads. Norman went up to his office and began making phone calls to the band, to the promoters—and to the insurance company to find out if the tour was covered to make up for all our losses.

As soon as the news got out, phone calls started coming in, especially from wives of the band members. One woman I had always looked up to said, "I believe that God has done this to you because you're getting too locked into who you think you are—you've taken God off the throne, so He has shut you up."

Then another woman called and said, "Look, Sheila, we just have to have enough faith. If you and I have enough faith, this tour can still go ahead." This kind of pressure was just too much. Again I broke my doctor's rule and talked in a low whisper, telling her, "Look, I've prayed. I've asked for healing, and it hasn't happened. The doctor says there's a growth. . . ."

My caller was like a Scottish terrier with her teeth in my leg—she just wouldn't let go. She kept saying, "Well, if you just have more faith, it will happen. . . ."

I Had to Get Alone with God

I realized I'd never be able to rest my voice in this kind of melée. I had to get away from well-meaning Christians and work all this out alone with God. Through our pastor, I found people in our church who were willing to let me use their small vacation home on the south coast of England.

I packed a bag with a few things and took our dog, Tilly, who would be my only companion during ten days of prayer and fasting at the little beach house. (Tilly was the only one I wanted to see during this time because she wagged her tail whether I sang or not.)

Norman drove me down and got me settled, but he didn't stay long. He had to get back to London to try and salvage what he could.

Soon I was alone, and, like Job, my first question was "Why?" I just couldn't understand. Didn't God realize what a big celebration He could have had in heaven after the tour was over and all those people had become Christians? What was going on? Were the band members' wives right? Did I think too much of myself? Didn't I have enough faith to trust God for healing?

For ten days I prayed, fasted, walked the beach, and asked God why. I tried to examine my life, and I kept wondering about those ominous words: *You may never sing again.* Is this what God had in mind? Singing had been my life. Ever since I graduated from London Bible College, one of my main goals had been to glorify God with my voice. I had served with British Youth for Christ. I had made records and done tours of Europe and America. I had sung everywhere, from giant cathedrals in Europe to tiny churches on the back roads of Kansas.

And now was it all over?

I had to wrestle with wondering whether I loved my singing ministry more than I loved Jesus Himself. After ten days of fasting and praying, I still had no answers, no revelation to take back home and help people to understand.

On the last morning of my stay, I went back out on the beach near the cottage to wait for Norman to come down and pick me up. As I watched the gentle waves roll in, I became aware of a blanket of God's love. I had run out of things to say, just as Job had. As I prayed I said to God, "Okay, I give up. If it's true that I love my career more than I love You—if I'm on some kind of ego trip—then please take it all away. *Don't give my voice back to me.*"

Until then I had never been willing to actually tell God I didn't need my voice back. But once I got the words out, it made all the difference. In the next few moments I got the distinct impression that God was saying, "Sheila, don't you

81

understand that I love you because of who you are and not for what you do? Your security has been all wrapped up in thinking of yourself as Sheila Walsh the singer, the evangelist, the speaker, the person who goes out there and does it all for Me. But that's not why I love you. If you never sing another note, it will not matter to Me. I don't need you to do things for Me. I just really love you."

As I stood there on the beach, vulnerable and empty-handed, I realized that at that moment I was richer than I'd ever dreamed. Christian service is a poor substitute for Jesus Himself. We must ask ourselves whether we want to run ourselves ragged doing things for God or to do the best part: be His friend.

God Has Many Servants but Few Friends

Out of my ten days of walking the beach, that was the only answer God gave me, but it was enough. I realized that for God there is a giant difference between servanthood and friendship. On the night before He died on the cross, Jesus told His disciples that He didn't want to call them servants. Now He wanted to call them friends because He had made known to them everything He had heard from His heavenly Father.[1]

Through that verse I could hear God telling me, "Sheila, I have many servants, but few friends. I have many people going places for Me, doing things for Me, but few who just love Me."

That thought burned into my heart and mind, and I determined to be one of God's friends, no matter what the cost.

It struck me that I had never asked God whether He wanted me to do the tour. I guess we had thought it would be sort of a surprise party for Him. Now I understood that

God was not interested in having me run around doing things for Him. He was interested in my friendship, my love, and my companionship.

To this day, I still don't understand everything about what happened. I don't understand why things went wrong and why some people were hurt because of the tour's cancellation. But one lasting impression has never faded: If I never made another album, if I never sang another song, if I were no longer "hot on the Christian charts"—it didn't matter. All that mattered was who I was to Jesus. That day I remembered something my mum had told me when I was just a young girl: "Who you are alone with Jesus—*that's who you really are.*"

That is so true for all of us. Who we are with Jesus Christ, our Savior and Friend, is who we really are. The public image doesn't matter. Who are we when we're alone with the Lord? The rest is empty rhetoric.

"Sheila, Your Throat Is Healed"

A couple of days after getting home, I reported back to my doctor as he had suggested. It had been just over two weeks since he had warned me not to talk. He took X-rays, and after looking at them, he turned to me with a puzzled expression. "Sheila, the growth is gone. It just isn't there anymore. I still suggest you go easy on talking for another week or two, but it looks as if your throat is healed."

I went home on cloud nine and sat down to put my feelings and thoughts into a song of some kind. Over the next few days, I started thinking about how trapeze performers start out needing a safety net. Later they become more confident, and the net is taken away. It was a spiritual picture of what I had done with my life. I had decided that I was far enough along to go it on my own, and I didn't need the

Trapeze

I was the only one, star of the show,
Thought I could make it on my own.
Then came the big surprise, out of the blue
What is a clown supposed to do?
Suddenly I'm falling out of the sky
Don't let me go, or I will die
Whose hands are these, on my trapeze
Take hold of me or there will be a tragedy.
Whose hands are these on my trapeze
I'm falling free, You rescued me
So willingly, on my trapeze.

Why did I walk away? You were my life
Patiently taught me how to fly
That was my big mistake, I need You so
Please hold me tight, don't let me go.[2]

safety net anymore. God had given me back my voice, but He had left me with a gentle warning.

I teamed with my friends and producers Jon Sweet and Rod Trott to write a song simply called "Trapeze." We all swing on our own trapeze, and sometimes we think we are the stars of the show, that we can make it on our own. We soon learn differently, however, but just as our fingers might be slipping off, a bigger, stronger hand grips us tightly and won't let us fall.

Serving God is important, even vital, but it should never come ahead of realizing that He is first of all our Friend, and without His friendship, life is an empty treadmill. Christianity is not an employer/employee contract; it is a relationship between a loving heavenly Father and His children.

Job: God's Servant and Friend

In the opening scenes of the story of Job, Satan accused Job of being God's servile employee because Job was getting a good deal. God disagreed, and this confrontation led to a great cosmic struggle between good and evil, played out in the life of one man.

Job's response to incredible disaster, pain, and suffering proves that he was more than simply a servant who had been living a righteous life because it paid off. After Satan's first attack, which killed Job's children and destroyed his wealth, Job still saw God as his Friend:

> I was naked when I was born.
>   And I will be naked when I die.
> The Lord gave these things to me. And he
>   has taken them away.
> Praise the name of the Lord. (Job 1:21)

Later, when horrible boils beset him and he was in terrible pain, Job's wife came to him and wondered why he was still trying to stay innocent after all that God had done to him. Why didn't he just curse God and die? Job's answer set a standard for every believer who wants to have a genuine friendship with God: "Should we take only good things from God and not trouble?" (Job 2:10).

Still later in the story, as Job was in the midst of his debates with his three friends, who tried to convince him that his sins had caused his suffering, Job admitted that he had a strong complaint because God's hand seemed to be heavy against him. He wanted to find God to present his case to Him. He knew that God would listen. Job said:

> But God knows the way that I take.
>   When he has tested me, I will come out
>   pure as gold.
> My feet have closely followed his steps.
>   I have stayed in his way without turning
>   aside.
> I have never left the commands he has
>   spoken.
>   I have treasured his words more than my
>   food. (Job 23:10–12)

Again and again in Job's story, we see that there is more between him and God than an employer/employee relationship. He was God's servant, true, but he was also God's friend. Throughout his entire ordeal, Job's reactions prove that he did not serve God for what he could get out of Him but for what he could give to Him from the very core of his being. Job did not serve God out of fear or duty. He served God out of love, and so it should be between friends.

At times it is easy for us to get caught up in Christian "service." We can become members of every committee and attend every prayer group. Wherever there is a job to be done in the church, we will be there. We may run ourselves ragged doing things for God and lose Him in the midst of it all.

Ultimately, only our loyalty to Him as a person and a friend will hold us when hell is on our backs. That's what I've learned, and so have a number of Christians I've met.

Dave Boyer Asked His Friend for Help

A few years later, when Dave Boyer got up to sing at a banquet Norman and I were attending, I had never really met him. I'd heard him sing a couple of times, but what he did that evening was remarkable. He began to share, not just the successes and the good things, but the struggles he had had in his life.

Many people present who knew Dave were aware of his story. Before he had ever come to the Lord, he had been in real trouble. But as he talked to us that night, he told us of his second struggle. After he had come to the Lord, he had battled the very things that had threatened to tear him apart before his conversion. And his grip on his own trapeze had almost slipped.

I was so impressed with Dave that evening that I invited him to be my guest on "Heart to Heart." Dave graciously agreed to come and share his story.

A few weeks later he was with us in Virginia Beach. When I interviewed him on the program, I was struck by how humble and genuine he was as he shared with our viewers the kind of life he led before he knew Jesus—and what happened later when he began to slip.

Dave grew up in a godly home and was active in the church his father pastored, singing in the choir and regularly attending other functions. He never took his relationship with Jesus seriously, however, and at age fifteen he began pursuing a career as a professional singer and entertainer.

By the age of eighteen he took the stage name "Joey Stevens" and began emceeing at the "500 Club" in Atlantic

City, where stars like Frank Sinatra, Dean Martin, Jerry Lewis, and Sammy Davis, Jr., became his heroes.

But the entire nightclub scene took its toll, and Dave's marriage began to suffer. He started drinking heavily and using drugs. At times he was abusive to his wife and daughter, and they finally separated.

Dave knew that deep inside something was very wrong, but he seemed powerless to deal with it. His father had been very important in his life, a very godly man. As Dave struggled amid all of his problems, his father died. Something snapped deep inside of Dave.

Dave found himself, late at night, walking toward the railroad tracks, where he planned to wait for a train to come and end his life. A small Methodist church he passed on the way brought back a flood of memories of his father's church. In despair, Dave fell on the church steps, ramming his head against the door and crying, "God, let me live for You—give me the strength somehow." In that moment of desperation, Dave somehow realized that God did love him as He loved all people, and Dave had a fleeting moment of feeling peace and security.

Dave made his way to a telephone and called his brother, who was pastoring their late father's church. They arranged to meet, and after praying for several hours with his brother, Dave committed his life to Jesus Christ for the first time.

God proceeded to do many miracles in his life. His dependence on drugs and alcohol ended. He was reunited with his wife and daughter, and together they began building a Christ-centered home.

To show his gratitude, Dave began to sing for the Lord and was soon Christian music's number-one big-band-style vocalist. Bookings poured in, and his schedule became extremely busy. He found himself, like many of us do, worn-out from traveling the Christian circuit. He seldom had a chance to sit down on Sundays in his own fellowship and receive spiritual nurture and support. Instead, he was always out somewhere else, helping to provide for everyone else.

Slowly, just a little at a time, Dave began drinking again. He turned away from his real Friend and began to rely on a comfortable old friend, which was no friend at all.

One night, a pastor sat down with Dave and asked, "Dave, how are you doing?"

Dave responded with the usual answer we all give when we want to cover up what's really going on inside: "Hey, I'm doing fine, Brother, thank you."

"No, Dave," his friend replied. "Now really, how are you doing?"

Dave could see he was at the end of the line, and so he opened up and cried out for help. At that moment God moved in and caught him before he fell completely. Just as his fingers were slipping, just as his grip was failing, the bigger, stronger hand of God caught him and would not let him fall.

We Can't Earn God's Friendship

As I listened to Dave tell his story, so many things were going through my mind. I thought of other people in responsible positions—pastors, teachers, and leaders—who so desperately need help but are unable to reach out and say, "Please help me! I'm in real trouble."

Too many Christians are enslaved by their own ministries, trapped into thinking they can't be real, honest, or open because that would undermine their testimony—and their status.

I marveled at how wonderful it was when Dave was able to reach out and ask for the help he needed. His story made me realize again that ministry *is* a poor substitute for Jesus' friendship.

As the broadcast ended, Dave stood up and began to sing "Calvary Covers It All." I sat in the quietness of the studio and just wept in gratitude for the fact that when we do blow it, when we fall flat on our faces, when we try and don't make it, *there is still a place to go*. Whether you are nine or ninety, whether you have known the Lord for two weeks or twenty years, you can always say to Him: "Why did I walk away? You were my life. You patiently taught me how to fly, and that was my big mistake. I thought I could fly on my own. But that isn't so. Please hold me tight. *Don't let me go!*"

That's what I was saying to God that day on the beach, when I faced the possibility of never singing again. I was asking Jesus for help. I knew I couldn't make it on my own. London's finest throat specialist had told me I might never sing again. But even more important at that moment, I didn't want to make it on my own. Whatever God had for me was fine. And just being His friend would be enough.

As it turned out, it was a valuable lesson I would need in the future. God healed my throat, but He did not heal my marriage. Storms lay ahead for Norman and me, and my resolve to stay on the altar would be tested to the limit.

Ship-Burning for Beginners: Laguna

When promises we have made
no longer seem to work or become too hard,
we can choose to walk away or to stay,
because we know we have made a covenant with God,
and He keeps His covenants with us.

Recently, my guests on "Heart to Heart" were Steve and Annie Chapman, who have written a book called *Married Lovers, Married Friends*. They started life together as married lovers, but had to learn how to be married friends. In the early years, they had many problems, mainly because each said "I do," while secretly thinking, "Well, maybe I do, and maybe I don't!"

As they worked out how to be a team rather than sparring partners, one thing that kept them together was remembering how they stood in a little Methodist church in a field in West Virginia years before and made their promises to stay together. Because they took those vows seriously, they were able to persevere when things got tough.

In their book, they have illustrated their commitment to each other with a story from the life of the Spanish explorer

91

Cortez. When he saw that his men were becoming uncertain and fearful about staying in a strange and unfamiliar land, Cortez gathered them on the shore and gave orders for them to set fire to all the ships on which they had sailed to Mexico. Now there would be no turning back. They were *committed*. Steve and Annie believe the same thing is true for every married couple: We need to burn our ships.

Before our interview ended, Steve and Annie sang the song that he had just written to illustrate what it means for a married couple to "burn their ships." One line in that song stays with me: "The ships are burning. There'll be no turning back for you and for me."

My Ship Stayed Anchored in the Bay

Almost one out of every two marriages in the United States is failing, and that includes a great many Christian marriages. It's pretty obvious that a lot of people go to the altar keeping their ships hidden in a cove somewhere, ready to sail away if things get a little too tough. I can speak from personal experience because after five years of marriage, I hadn't burned my ship. And I was almost ready to get on and sail away—anywhere—to escape my frustration and disappointment.

But no one really knew that—not even Norman, who went along blissfully for the most part, thinking everything was okay. I complained now and then, but I guess he thought that was to be expected, and it didn't bother him. He never detected my real discontent and disillusionment.

On several occasions I tried to convince Norman to go with me for marriage counseling, and once or twice I had even made the appointment. But the night before, he would say, "Please, do we have to do this? I know we can work it out." And then, because he really seemed to want to work it

The Ships Are Burning

We made this journey,
We sailed here together.
We made a promise
To stay here forever.
When we reached the shore
We kissed the ground.
You took my hand and we turned around,
And we smiled while we watched the flames
Light up the night.
'Cause the ships are burning.
There'll be no turning back
For you and for me.

Too many lovers are keeping their ships anchored in the bay.
One by lonely one we've seen them sail away.
But when we reached those shores
We kissed the ground,
You took my hand and we turned around
And we smiled while we watched the flames
Light up the night.
O, the ships are burning.

Chorus:
There'll be no turning back, for you and me.
Whatever we find here,
We've made it clear,
Here is where we'll always be.
On this island of pleasure
There'll be some dangers,
And we might think about returning,
But we both know we won't go.
That's why, I know that's why
The ships are burning
I know that's why, I know that's why
The ships are burning.[1]

out, we'd cancel the appointment, and things would go on much as they had before.

In my frustration and anger, I began living two lives. There was my outer life, where everybody could see that I was faithful and obedient to my husband. But I had another life in my mind, where I would look at other men and think, *I wonder what life would have been like if I had married him?* Sometimes I would lie in bed at night and play out little scenes in my mind, imagining that I wasn't Norman's wife anymore, but that I belonged to some other man instead. Of course, the other man was always kind and romantic and wonderful.

I had my own private joke on Norman because he didn't know a thing about my secret life. I thought it was safe—a game a Christian woman could play without much risk. After all, I wasn't harming anybody, and nobody knew what I was doing but me. I was still saying enough of the right words to make everybody believe I was a good wife, but in my mind I had a way of escape, an area that only I controlled.

Of course, my escapist fantasies never remotely turned into reality. I had no desire to be unfaithful to Norman. I just had the Christian equivalent of being unfaithful, which I thought was harmless enough. It never occurred to me that I was playing with fire. I lived in a foolish Cinderella world.

We Moved Our Battle to Laguna Beach

By 1986 we were performing more and more concerts in the United States, and it became clear that we should make America our base of operations. Billy Ray Hearn, president of Sparrow Records and our good friend, suggested that we live in his beach house in Laguna Beach, California, for a while before deciding where we wanted to settle. It sounded great to us. In fact, we had stayed in that same beach house briefly on one of our tours, and I remembered how beautiful it was.

After we got to California, things improved—at times. After all, Laguna Beach is a very romantic spot, and even during our most difficult moments I never doubted that Norman believed he loved me. *He* really seemed happy and content. He just didn't realize that I didn't feel loved. I began to experience a tremendous restlessness, as if I were tapping my fingers on my life, waiting for something to happen and not knowing what it was.

It didn't take long for us to start arguing again, and I soon started feeling desperate. Steam started to escape from the teakettle, especially when Norman would say things like "People told me that you were like this—your friends told me you were like this."

"Like what?" I demanded.

"Oh, unreasonable, terrible temper, explosive . . . I should have known."

Conversations like that drove me absolutely wild. It was as if Norman had invited everyone I had ever worked with or cared for into his camp and left me on the other side of a thick wall by myself. I felt as if I were being backed farther and farther up against that wall and that one day something inside me would snap.

I would complain to Norman that we didn't have a normal marriage. "People don't live this way," I sighed.

"Of course, they do," he reasoned. "You have this ridiculous expectation of what marriage really is like. If you knew the truth, you'd see that there are far more people like us than you realize."

I didn't believe that, and I said so, adding, "I'd rather live by myself than live with you and be as miserable as this."

At that time, I meant every word. I felt we had no intimacy

in our marriage. To me, intimacy was far more than sex. It was a communion between two people who could really talk and share their lives, their joys, their happiness, and their concern for each other. I didn't think Norman and I had any of that. All I ever heard him saying, basically, was "Look, just go out there and sing, and I'll take care of everything else."

But I wanted more than that. I wanted him to talk to me, to tell me what he thought. Did Norman ever worry about things? Did he have any fears? I never felt that he shared anything from the inside.

I Didn't Realize How Norman Felt

One night we sat in a lovely restaurant called The Cottage in Laguna. It was a balmy summer evening, and we had an outside table. I thought, *Okay, we've been home from the road for a week now, and Norman can't use his usual excuse that I always nag when he's really tired and under pressure. I'm going to try to talk to him right now, and I'm even willing to admit it's all my fault. But no matter whose fault it is, we need help because I'm really miserable.*

I started talking to Norman about how unhappy I was with our marriage. I tried to be calm and matter-of-fact, but I could see he was getting angry. I didn't realize what was going on inside of him in a conversation like that. I never fully understood how deeply affected he had been by his mother's death. I had not experienced the loneliness and desertion he felt when he packed his bags and left home while still a teenager.

Even more crucial, however, was the fact that I had no inkling of how the collapse of his first marriage had eaten at him. He had become ill because he felt like such a failure. But I knew none of that. As I talked on, Norman was sitting

96

there thinking I was slipping out of his grasp. He couldn't deal with my questions because he didn't have any answers.

Instead of having a discussion, we were soon in a heated argument. I interpreted Norman's anger as simply not caring, not wanting to listen to me. We got into the car and roared out of the parking lot, screaming down Pacific Coast Highway at 85 m.p.h. He was really upset and wouldn't respond when I begged him to slow down. I thought, *He's going to kill us. If he hits something, we haven't got a hope.*

We screeched up to the house and got out of the car. He slammed the car door and then slammed the front door to the house. Then he went to the bedroom and slammed that door as well. I followed him into the house and sat on the couch, not even bothering to turn on the lights. I sobbed for what seemed like hours. I was sure that sooner or later he'd be coming through that door to say he was sorry. *Surely* he couldn't sleep after this! But I sat there all night until sunrise, and Norman never came through that door. He just went to bed and, I guessed, to sleep.

At 7:00 the next morning, he came out of the bedroom and found me sitting there. If I looked half as desolate as I felt, I must have been a sorry sight.

"Morning," he said congenially. "Can I make you a cup of tea?"

As he left for his office in Laguna Niguel, he smiled and said, "Bye. . . . See you later."

That was the day something in me died. I thought, *I don't know why I'm doing this. I'm the only one who is hurting—the only one who feels anything. He doesn't feel a thing; he just doesn't care.* What I didn't realize was that Norman was hurting almost as much as I was, but he was afraid to open up Pandora's Box because if he did, there was no way he could get everything back in again.

In the heat of our argument in The Cottage restaurant,

Norman had said, "I know you'll never leave me because it will ruin your reputation, and you could never do concerts again."

I began to think that I didn't care if I ever did concerts again. The present situation was destroying me, literally destroying me. I thought I'd rather get a job somewhere, just go and find a church and say to the pastor, "Look, I've made a mess of my life. Can I just be a member here?" I would get some kind of a job and find a life where I could have peace.

I Began to Plan My Escape

On the day after our Cottage restaurant blow-up, I began to lay my plans. I would take my time, but I would find a way to get out of this. I wouldn't tell Norman because he didn't deserve that much; I had tried to tell him for five years. In the beginning I had thought it was equally my fault as well as his. And for all I knew right now, it was all my fault, but I didn't care anymore. I had tried to ask him for help, and he hadn't listened. Now I secretly planned to get away from him. One morning he'd wake up, and I would just be gone.

Even as I write these words, I am completely aware that all the things I remember, all the pictures that dance before my eyes, are filtered through my heart and my memory. I know that if you sat down and had dinner with Norman, you would hear it all from a different viewpoint. In the midst of our struggle, it seemed to me as if he didn't care, but now I know that he cared very much. When I felt he wasn't listening, he was hearing every word. But I just didn't realize it because I was too busy trying to survive.

During the following weeks I became polite and very cool. I cooked all of Norman's meals, ironed his shirts, did the concerts, smiled and shook hands with people. Oddly enough, up on the stage, trying to help people who were hurting, I felt real. In a way, I was being a hypocrite, as Norman often pointed out, but at the same time I could still talk to people about pain and hurting because *I knew exactly how they felt*. After concerts, people would come up. We would pray together, and I would cry with them. Ironically, in my "hypocrisy," I found the only place where I could be "real."

Of course, I could never tell anyone my real problems. Everyone wanted me to be doing just fine, thank you, because I was a Christian artist, the one who talked about Jesus' love and how to hang onto the Lord. That summer we went to a Christian artists' seminar in Colorado, where a promoter friend of mine started telling me about all the Christian leaders whose marriages were falling apart. He said, "You know, Sheila, you're about the only hope I've got left. If you ever fell apart, I think it would destroy me."

I looked at him, not able to say anything, but realizing that here was a man who thought there would be no way my marriage could ever be in trouble. He could trust Sheila Walsh because she was solid. There were a lot of flakes out there, but Sheila would always be reliable.

I didn't realize it then, but my friend's words would play a major part in my healing. They would speak to me again and again, reminding me that my decisions could affect many people. One day I would have to answer for my choices, and as the Scriptures teach, privilege brings great responsibility.[2]

Nonetheless, I remained distant, and Norman started to sense that I had changed. "What's wrong with you?" he'd ask. "You're so cold."

"Why, no," I'd respond evenly. "Nothing's wrong. I'm fine, thank you."

But as my cool, detached attitude continued, Norman began to say, "Look, you know, maybe you have been right. Maybe we need to get some help."

But by now I was in no mood for counseling.

"Norman, if you think you need some counseling, that's fine. I don't need any counseling. I'm just fine, thank you."

But Norman insisted that we try a counselor. He must have sensed that I had built a wall around myself and that there was no way he could begin to penetrate it. I finally agreed to go, but reluctantly, because I knew what was going to happen. We would go to a counselor, and Norman would unload on my head as he had done so many times in the past. Emotionally, I was feeling about two feet tall, and I could see Norman telling the counselor what a terrible person I was and the counselor agreeing and trying to pummel me into submission.

The Counselor Surprised Me

I was wrong. The counselor let both of us talk, and the first session went quite well. I came home thinking, *Well, maybe this isn't all my fault. Maybe there are two sides to this after all. . . .*

In the second session we were given a temperament analysis test. I was extremely wary of the results. I felt that Norman was waiting to get some official proof that I was a real nut case and that a trained counselor had proven it, and now we had it in writing.

But when the results came back, the counselor said, "Sheila, you need to work on your self-discipline, but basically you're doing okay. Norman, you are *extremely* disciplined. Do you feel a need to control Sheila?"

I sat there, listening in amazement. I couldn't believe that we both had areas to work on. All along I thought the counseling was for my benefit, that I was the naughty little kid who had been dragged in for misbehaving at school.

"Well," Norman replied, hesitantly, "no. . . . What do you mean?"

100

"I mean," our counselor replied, "are you trying to tighten your grip on Sheila because you feel you're losing her?"

"I don't think so . . . I don't want to control her . . . I . . ." Norman started to cry right there in the counselor's office.

I had seen Norman cry only once, several years before. We had gone to see the film *Ordinary People,* which starred Mary Tyler Moore as a mother who rejected her son. Norman's tears had surprised me, but he had brushed it off as "a good movie that had gotten to him." What I didn't realize was how much the film reminded him of his own childhood—the death of his mother and how much he missed her.

When Norman was able to continue, he admitted, "You know, I just feel that everything is falling apart, and there's nothing I can do."

That was a start, but it didn't change my basic "dead inside" feeling. In one of our sessions, the counselor asked me, "Do you want this marriage to work?"

"No, I don't," I answered.

"Well, why are you here?" the counselor asked.

"Because Norman asked me to come."

"Are you prepared to give it a chance?" the counselor asked, gazing intently at me.

"I really don't know. I would like to think I am, but I feel five years beyond help. I think that if I'd seen you five years ago it might have done some good. I've done everything I know how to do to give it a chance, and now I don't know if I still care anymore."

I Wasn't the Only Casualty

Nonetheless, we stayed with it—a counseling session every Tuesday at 10:00 in the morning. Despite my anger and pain, I began to see that I wasn't the only casualty in this war. I learned that Norman had feelings, that he actually cared, and that he had been deeply hurt by some of the hateful things I had said to him to get him to react. He started feeding some of these back during counseling, things like "I hate you; I wish I'd never married you."

And it was true. I had said those things to him more than once, especially when our arguments had erupted into fights, but it always looked to me as if it just rolled off his back. I felt as if I were throwing a teaspoon of oil into an ocean.

I remember in particular a concert in Vancouver, British Columbia. As usual, our schedule was more than hectic. We'd gotten up at 4:00 A.M. and flown in from somewhere, and I wanted to go to the hotel to rest for an hour before the concert. But Norman wanted me to do another radio interview to help with promotion. I'd already done four radio interviews that day, and I said, "Norman, can't we skip this one? I simply have to get some rest."

"Look, Sheila, this is important, and I think you need to do it."

I stared at Norman with a look of disbelief and finally said, "Do you ever take your hat off as my manager long enough to be a husband and see me as your wife? *Can't you see I'm exhausted?* All I want is an hour—someplace to go and just be quiet."

Norman didn't even seem to hear. He just responded, "Look, this guy has set up an interview. He's spent a lot of time organizing it, and you should be there. You said you'd do it, and you should honor your word."

"You know, Norman," I said, "you care more about the guy doing the radio interview than you do about me. You're more concerned for him than you are for me."

"Don't be ridiculous, Sheila. You just feel sorry for yourself."

By now I was angry and started to cry. Norman said, "Good grief! Don't go off on one of those things again."

102

I Felt Like a Leaf in the Wind

Whenever he felt I was getting out of control, Norman would say, "You're such a hypocrite. You stand up there on the stage, and you talk about God's love and about the fruit of the Spirit, and now look at you. If people could see you now, they would never listen to another word that came out of your mouth."

When Norman said things like that, I started to crumble. I felt that as he talked I was becoming like a leaf, that if he said one more word I would blow away in the wind and there would be nothing left.

My perceptions of our arguments and fights may make Norman sound cold and uncaring, but that really isn't true. Norman works hard. At times we have faced tremendous financial pressures. He worries about paying his bills. He is impeccably honest, a man of his word.

But driving Norman even harder was a desire to see me succeed. It wasn't that he wanted me to make a lot of money. It's just that he believed God had given me a gift—not only of singing but also of being able to share God's love with people. He would watch me sit for hours after concerts, talking to people and seeing that they were helped, and he'd tell me, "I can't do that, Sheila. That just blows me away. You have a tremendous gift."

With his disciplined approach to everything, Norman just thought that I should be in as many places as I could and give as much of myself as possible. Understandably, I thought it was a bit ironic when Norman said in the counselor's office, "It's so funny. You help everybody else in the world, and you destroy me."

I stared at Norman in shock. *I* was destroying him? Norman went on, "You know, Sheila, I feel as if we're two birds on a branch, and every time one of us tries to gather enough strength to try its wings, the other one claws it back down again."

The counseling continued for over two months, but nothing seemed to get any better. This was not only frustrating to Norman, but it was frightening as well. He was in the mood to try to make the marriage work, but I was slipping through his fingers.

"You're not even giving it a try," he'd tell me. "You're not even prepared to try anymore."

"Norman, I tried for years, and you wouldn't begin to try. So now we've been going to counseling for two months, and you're angry because I won't try. Come to me five years from now, after you've tried for five years yourself, and maybe I'll listen to you."

I was in no mood for reason or logic. I felt I had a good case against Norman, and I wasn't going to let him off the hook.

Our Marriage Hung by a Thread

Every day the walls of my trap seemed to grow deeper and more slippery. I got the feeling that Norman was thinking, *Sheila, if you leave me, I'll be fine because I'll keep going. You're the one who will fall apart. Where will you go? What will you do?*

I wondered that myself. I had nowhere to go, nowhere to run. Yet, the promise I had to made to Norman and to God had become too hard, I thought, and I wanted to give up. I had loved God all my life, and I'd never gotten involved with alcohol or drugs. I never slept with anyone before I married Norman. I had always wanted to do it God's way.

Now I decided I'd had enough. I was tired of it all. I was tired of always making the right choices.

I looked around me to see if anyone else was struggling the way I was. Was anyone winning his or her battle with

Satan? No one I knew, I decided. One friend was on her second divorce and was thanking God for the provision of a third husband. Another friend stood up on stage to preach the gospel, and then went back to his room to drink himself into oblivion.

I thought, *This makes no sense to me! Maybe I've held onto a ridiculous standard. After all, we're all human. We all have needs and desires. We all fall flat on our faces from time to time. Maybe I need to blow it. Maybe I need to make some real mistakes, so I can come back to the Lord and understand what it really means to be forgiven.*

I had had enough of my husband. I was going to walk away from him.

Norman accurately perceived me as the one who had taken control. In the counselor's office, he once said, "I feel that our marriage is hanging by a thread, and you're standing over it with a big pair of scissors."

And so we continued like that, hanging by a thread until the Christmas holidays. I decided I'd had enough, and I wanted to fly home to Scotland for Christmas.

"I want to go to Scotland and be by myself, and I'd rather you didn't come with me."

"How can we possibly spend Christmas apart? We've never done that."

"Well, I'll go up and see my mum, and then I'll come back down to London and see you on Christmas Day. But right now, I want to go home, and I need to be alone."

"Okay, if that's what you want, that's what we'll do."

We flew into London, and I went up to Scotland while Norman stayed with Gerald and Anona Coates in London. I told Mum everything—what a mess our marriage was, what a mess I was, and there was no way it could be fixed.

Mum didn't say much. She just listened and told me that she'd pray for both of us.

No counseling, no advice, no condemning Norman because he had treated her little girl so badly. Mum was a good listener, and she loved Norman.

I went back down to London, and we spent a miserable Christmas Day together. Making it more miserable was the fact that we had to pretend to Gerald and Anona that we were doing all right. Norman wanted to say something, but I said, "Absolutely not. If you start talking, I'm gone. . . . I'm leaving. . . . I'll meet you at the airport."

So Norman kept silence, and I kept thinking, *When I wanted to talk to them, you didn't want to talk. Now you want to ask for help because we're falling apart. Let's just get back home so I can work out how I'm going to get away from you.*

The Stalemate Continued

When we got back to Laguna Beach, we resumed counseling, but it seemed as though we had hit a stalemate. The counselor made it clear that I had no grounds for divorce— neither of us did. Norman had not been unfaithful to me, nor had I been unfaithful to him. What we needed to do was work this thing through, and with God's help the counselor felt it was possible. I can recall his saying, "If you only knew how many people have sat in the chairs you are sitting in now who never thought they would make it, but they did make it."

But they wanted it to work. I don't want it to work. Maybe God can make it work, but I don't want it to work. I've had it!

And Norman would sit there, looking at me with eyes that wanted me to say, "I love you." He wanted me to say all the things I had been trying to say for the past five years. But I just couldn't.

Sometimes, when Norman drove up to Los Angeles on business, I would imagine that he was coming home down the San Diego Freeway and that there was an accident. I imagined sitting there and hearing a knock at the door. I'd open it, and there would be a highway patrol officer to tell me that Norman was gone.

Then I'd stop myself. *Just think about that for a minute. You open the door, and there's the police officer, and Norman's gone. Suddenly you realize you really did care for him. Now it's too late, and you'll never be able to forgive yourself. You'll never be able to say you're sorry.*

Later, when I finally did hear Norman's key in the lock and saw him walk in, I felt a mixture of relief and turmoil.

I was torn with wanting him gone and still caring about him as a person. There were nights when we would sit on the balcony, and I would just hold Norman in my arms because he felt so desperate and alone.

Not Even God Could Help Us Now

By this time, much of my anger had boiled away, and I felt as if I were grieving for something that was dead. Sometimes I would say, "You know, I'm sorry. I never wanted to hurt you like this."

We would sit and be sad together, and I kept thinking, *I wish you had felt this way a long time ago, because I believe we could have salvaged it then. Now not even God can help.*

While I thought that not even God could help our marriage, I never felt He was judging me. I felt as though He hurt for me and that He was one of the few people I could talk to. And I knew He hurt for Norman, too, because Norman would tell me, "It would be a disaster if we got divorced."

Mentally I ran through what I would tell Norman if I ever did leave: *You think it will be a disaster, but God will take care of it. God loves you and understands you. I don't understand you, but He does. God loves me, and you're trying to tell me I'll be lost as a*

Christian if I leave you, but I won't. I know it's not the right thing, but it's the only thing I can do. I don't have anywhere left to go. It's all I can do. And I know that God loves me enough to be there for me.

One day in late April, Norman said, "I think we need to get away for a vacation."

We had friends who had often offered us their villa on Kauai in the Hawaiian Islands. Norman suggested we take them up on the offer, and I said, "Why not?" It sounded restful, and I decided not to take any Christian books with me—not even a Bible. I'd just go lie in the sunshine. I didn't even want to think anymore.

As we flew to Kauai, I was torn by conflicting emotions. I was still determined that I was going to get away, that I would go ahead and leave Norman. Yet, I also knew that I had no grounds for divorce. I had searched through the Christian bookstores to find something that would let me off the hook, but there wasn't anything theologically sound.

I had talked to friends who had divorced their husbands, and there was an emptiness. I knew that they had paid dearly for their "freedom."

I also thought of all the kids who believed in me, who felt that if I could make it, they could make it. For twenty-two years I had been a Christian, and now the rubber was meeting the road. If God couldn't help me now, then none of this would make sense. In a way, I'd never really needed God before. Oh, I had needed His comfort and strength, but I had never been at a place where my will ran smack into the face of His will.

When you try to hold onto heaven with hell on your back, it often comes down to your will or God's. I had promised to love, cherish, and obey Norman in a covenant with him and God. Now I was faced with one of those critical choices: Would I choose to walk away from that promise to Norman and to God, or would I keep the covenant because God had always kept His covenants with me?

I didn't know. Could God trust me? Could I trust Him? I had to find out whether Christianity worked or not.

S I X

Ship-Burning for Beginners: Kauai

Norman and I landed in Kauai and settled into the villa for a twelve-day stay. He went his way, to a tennis court where he played most of the day, and I went mine, to walk the beach, to pray, and to think.

I looked back on a lot of points in my life where I had made choices. I thought of the times when I had run to grab hold of God's feet and hang on. Now, after all these years, was I just going to walk away? I knew without a shadow of a doubt that if I did what I wanted to do, I would walk away.

Friends of mine in the Christian music industry had told me that divorce wouldn't be that bad. I could get away with it. All I had to do was lay low for about six months, and people would forget. They also told me they never thought Norman and I were very well suited, that I'd find someone else because I was still young.

In my heart of hearts it all sounded like lies. None of it sounded as if it came from heaven. It came from the pit of

111

hell. But the trouble was that I was tired of holding on, and I felt so alone.

It was as if I had everything in a basket in front of me, but I just didn't want what was in that basket anymore. One set of voices kept saying, *You've got to find yourself—now. You have to go after your own happiness, or you'll be miserable and resent Norman for the rest of your life.*

So I walked the beach every day, and the Lord walked by my side, not speaking, only listening. I talked to Him every day, but I never felt He condemned me. He just walked along beside me and listened.

I kept asking, *What do I do?* I knew Norman was hurting, and I knew he was lonely and scared. Just before we left for Kauai he said, "I'll do anything . . . *anything*. I know I've blown it. I know I never listened when I should have listened. I really love you, and I'll do anything to make it work."

I had to admit that Norman had changed his attitude, but mine seemed set in cement. One morning during our first week in Kauai, Norman showed me a book. It was called *This Present Darkness,* and the author was a man named Frank Peretti. I remembered that it had arrived at the villa a few days before, addressed to me by one of our friends who had learned where we had gone. I had glanced at the cover and tossed it aside, not interested in reading anything. But Norman had picked it up and read it, and that morning at breakfast he said, "I think you'd like this book—it's really interesting."

One evening, just as our vacation was ending, I came across the book again around 7:00 at night. I began reading, and the first time I looked up it was 10:00. I just wasn't able to put the book down. Norman said, "I'm going up to bed. Are you coming?"

"I'll be there in a little while. I just want to read a little more."

I continued reading on and on through the night. Peretti's novel is based on Ephesians 6:12: "Our fight is not against people on earth. We are fighting against the rulers and authorities and the powers of this world's darkness. We are fighting against the spiritual powers of evil in the heavenly world."

The book was a spiritual allegory of sorts with the action taking place in a typical small town. The angels were watching to see what choices people would make. And, of course, the demons were at work, throwing things in people's faces and laughing at them when they slipped and failed.

In one scene, the demons brought a seductive young woman across the path of a sincere young minister. Then they stood back to see what he would do. As she tried to entice him, they goaded her on, speaking through her and whispering in his ear.

Peretti's Story Was My Story

As I read on through the night, I began to apply what was happening in Peretti's novel to what was happening in our marriage. I could see that the demons were always at work, wanting us to do what felt good. But I knew that I'd entered into a covenant with God and that I would never find peace if I did what felt good at the moment, which was to run.

So how long would you run, Sheila?

Just twenty-four hours before, I had been walking the beach. At one place I had fallen on my face in the sand, crying out to God, "You've got to help me because I have nothing left. I have no strength left to choose Your will. I can see Your will up there, it's hanging in front of me, and I don't have any strength left to reach up and grab it. I want to be able to do it, but I can't. You've got to help me because I'm in real trouble, and I don't know what to do! Lord, please help me. I want to do the right thing."

Dawn was starting to faintly streak the sky as I neared the conclusion of *This Present Darkness*. The story had focused on a small band of faithful people who were experiencing incredibly vicious attacks by demonic hordes. At one point an angel looked down to see what was going on in the town as the demons were running amok, and he said, "Why don't we move in and destroy them?"

But another angel said, "We can't. Nobody's praying. If we went in there now we would be wiped out."

Not long after that, an old woman in the story became so disturbed about what was happening in the little town that she got out of bed and got down on her knees to pray, and then prayed some more. Through the strength of prayers like hers, the angels were empowered to destroy the demonic forces.

The demons were defeated because a few faithful people stood firm in the face of ridiculous odds. The story ended with a small band of believers experiencing tremendous victory through the choices they made, the stand they took, and, above all, their prayers.

As I read the last chapters of the book, everything became clear. The Lord was allowing me to see what was really happening. In the twenty-two years I had been a Christian, I had daily embraced God's will and marched bravely forward with Him, but now it was my own time to know just how Job had felt.

The devil told God, "Now wonder Job loves You, his life is a dream—a nice family, very affluent, successful. Take all that away, and You've lost him." But God said, "No, it won't happen because Job's a friend of mine." God staked His reputation on the life of one man and then stood back to watch what would happen.

And then it occurred to me that the same was true now. Everybody was watching—God, the angels, Satan, my friends, and the thousands of people who knew me through my concerts and records. They were all watching to see what I was going to do after all the blessing that had been invested in my life. I had come within a hairsbreadth of slapping God in the face and saying, "Sorry, but You're going to have to lose this one!"

I put down the book, pulled my wallet out of my purse, and dug out a crumpled and worn copy of my marriage vows. Norman and I had written those vows together, and I looked at the words again:

> I take you, Norman, to be my husband, believing this to be God's will and purpose.
> I will love you, comfort you, honor, and obey you.
> I will love you and cherish you in every circumstance of life, whether you be well or ill, strong or weak, 'til death parts us, and before God I pledge to you my faithful support.
> And so I give you my promise.

As I read those words again it came to me: *These are my words. This is the covenant I entered into, not just with Norman but with God. I made this covenant.*

"Satan—You've Lost!"

The sun was starting to peek out of the ocean as I finished the book, slapped it shut, and went outside the villa to the beach. I had made my decision. It may sound melodramatic now, but I actually dug my heels into the sand and addressed the enemy. I suppose I should have thanked God, but it was really important to me to say what I said to the king of demons himself: "I know who you are, and I know what you've been trying to do. I know you would love to destroy my life and destroy my marriage and my ministry, but I just want you to know that you can't do this, because I'm not my own; I'm God's daughter. Jesus paid for me with a price. And I want you to know right now that, like it or not, I'm going to go God's way and do His will, and I just wanted to be the first person to tell you that you have lost."

I'm not sure why I made that speech aloud. It would have appeared that only the waves were listening, but I knew someone was listening, and it was important for me to say what I said to him. Even though the promise I had made to God and Norman had seemed to be too hard, I had decided to stay, because I had made a covenant with a God Who kept His covenants with me.

Instead of walking away from Norman, I turned around, came through a door, and closed it behind me. With that decision, I turned toward Norman. He was still far away from me, but I had taken my first step back toward him. I knew it wouldn't be easy. It wasn't a "quick fix," but I had chosen my path.

Because of what happened to me on that beach, I know beyond any doubt that you *can* hold onto heaven with hell on your back. You can do that whether you are in the public eye on television, or whether you're an eighty-two-year-old woman from Phoenix, suffering from arthritis, not knowing how to pay your bills, but still faithfully following Christ.

For every Christian everywhere who attempts to do business with God, there will be a Gethsemane. There will be a time and a place where you have to let go of everything. I've often heard people say that the Crucifixion was the most important moment in history, and I suppose from a theological standpoint that's true. But I think an even more important moment in many ways was Jesus' praying in the Garden of Gethsemane because Jesus faced the fact that *He didn't want to go through pain and suffering*. He shrank from the cross, but nonetheless He said, "Father, I'll do it because I love You."

Jesus didn't simply give in and do the right thing. He chose to put aside His own will and embrace completely His Father's will instead.[1] My struggles to stay in my marriage gave me a taste of what that is like, and I thank God for what I learned.

"Norman, I Won't Walk Away"

After I gave Satan the news that he had lost, I came back into the house from the beach, freshened up, and made some breakfast. I could hear God saying to me, "You've made your commitment. You say you've closed the door on walking away. Now I want you to tell Norman that."

Norman came down, grabbed a bite to eat, and was headed out for the tennis courts when I said, "When you get back, can we go out to lunch? I need to talk to you."

Norman gave me a bit of a surprised look and said, "Sure, see you around 11:30."

We went to a lovely outdoor restaurant, and even before we ordered I said, "Norman, I want you to know that something happened to me last night. I want you to know that I'm not going to leave you. I also want you to know that I don't feel any different right now, but I'm in this with you, and I won't walk away."

I went on to tell Norman about my reading Peretti's book and finally having it become so clear. Sometimes we think we have no choice. We think we're backed into a corner, but I realized I did have a choice—that Jesus bought my choice for me on the cross.

Norman sat there listening, saying very little. When I stopped talking, he reached down and took my hand gently in his and said, "I know it's going to take a long, long time, but I really do love you."

We flew home the next day. On the plane, Norman commented that we would just have to start from scratch with our marriage. I agreed because I didn't think we ever had a real foundation to build upon before.

Norman and I still had two weeks before having to do a concert, so we started laying our new foundation by going out on dates. As we began leaving time for ourselves instead of pouring everything into work, we could see a difference almost immediately. Norman would take me out to dinner, and instead of fighting and driving wildly down the highway, we would just talk.

He listened when I told him of my needs and my dreams, and then he would share his feelings, particularly about how his mother's death had affected him. Slowly, we began to rebuild our communication lines.

And Then the "700 Club" Called

We'd been home for a little over a month and had just been out to dinner with friends when we came back to an answering machine message from Jackie Mitchum at the "700 Club": "Sheila, could you come into the '700 Club' next week and cohost for three days?"

I looked at Norman, and he looked at me. "Why does Jackie want me to cohost? I mean, is everybody away?"

The next morning Norman phoned Jackie and asked, "We got your message, can you tell us a little bit more?"

"Well, if Sheila could just come in for the three days it would be great. We're looking for the right person to be Pat's cohost."

I thought it would be fun and agreed to come. A couple of months before I had done a concert in Canada and had appeared on "100 Huntley Street," singing and speaking. What I didn't know was that Jackie had seen the show. In fact, she taped it and showed it to Pat Robertson. When Pat saw the video, he said, "This may be the girl we've been looking for."

They had been without a permanent cohost for almost a year and had tried several different people, but nobody had worked out. When we arrived, Nancy Kondas, the "700 Club" producer, met us and made everything clear: "We're looking for someone to be Pat's permanent cohost, and we hope you'd like to try out for the job."

I didn't know what to say. Here Norman and I were, just starting to put our marriage back together, and I was supposed to go on national television and become the associate of Pat Robertson? What if I took the job and a few months down the road our marriage fell apart? Think of all the damage that might do.

Feeling ambivalent, I told Nancy that I appreciated the opportunity. I was sure, however, that after I had blundered around for three days, they would decide that I wasn't the one.

I was whisked into an empty studio, where I sat in a chair, reading something from a teleprompter. I thought it was so strange to practice what you were going to be saying. Then they brought in one of the research assistants, sat her down, and told me to practice interviewing her. So there we both sat, feeling stupid as I interviewed the poor woman about nothing in particular.

The next morning I had to show up early to meet Pat in his dressing room—that is, after I had gone through makeup at 7:30 A.M. To be truthful, I didn't like the way I looked. There I was, with a Christian hairdo, lots of makeup, wearing a dress I didn't like, and thinking, *What on earth am I doing here?* Suddenly a little red light went on, and we were live across the country before millions of viewers.

"Sheila, You're the One for the Job"

As the show started, I thought all I would basically do was pray for people and perhaps talk with someone who had met the Lord under dramatic circumstances. Not so. Early during that first broadcast, the "Club" ran a piece about the West Bank and what was happening between the Arabs and the Jews. Pat turned and asked me what I thought about the situation. Deciding I didn't know enough to be the Connie Chung of Christian television, I replied, "To be honest with you, I don't know the difference between the West Bank and the Bank of America."

Poor Pat. There he sat, a gifted, intelligent, godly man, wondering what he should do with this unpredictable woman! Then he just smiled, turned to a map of the Middle East, and graciously explained the situation to me and to all our viewers.

After the first day, Pat invited Norman and me out for lunch. "You know, Sheila," he said, "I believe you're the person for the job. I believe that you're God's provision."

Norman and I felt that way too—even then. We felt as if "700 Club" were home. I told Norman later in the hotel, "When I walked in the door there, I felt as if I had just put on an old pair of slippers. But can I take this job after all we've just been through? We can't tell them—we don't even know them."

We flew back to California with the understanding that I would be back in two weeks, ready to go to work on the first of August. Because I was still not completely sure about taking the job, we went back to see our marriage counselor. We told him everything that had happened on Kauai. We knew we wanted to start again, but we were in for the long haul, and now I'd been invited to become cohost of the "700 Club."

"This is really bizarre. What should I do?" I asked. "Should I tell them that I'm sorry, but I can't come?"

The counselor smiled and said, "Maybe God's giving you a divine opportunity. Maybe He's pushing you to live out your decision. I think you should go for it."

Norman and I prayed about it together, and afterward I felt as if God were saying, "Okay, you've closed that door, Sheila. Pick up your feet and get on with life."

Our Tale of Two Cities Began

We returned to our place in Laguna Beach and made our plans. Norman had a lot of business pending in Nashville, and he felt that he really needed to spend two months taking care of things there. Having decided to accept the "700 Club" offer, I would have to live somewhere in Virginia Beach, so I could do the show each day.

We packed all our belongings in garbage bags, hauled them down to a temporary storage garage, and then prepared to fly in two directions—Norman to Nashville, where he was committed to at least two months' worth of business, and I to Virginia Beach to start my new life with the "700 Club."

Pat Robertson and the rest of the staff were wonderful. For the first month of so, I lived in a hotel until I found an apartment, and somebody loaned me a car until I bought one of my own.

Looking back, I can see that God provided our "tale of two cities" situation to help us get our new start. Norman and I had never really had an engagement, and now we were starting all over again, but gingerly. Although we had been "dating" and trying to cut down on work, I still wasn't sure I could ever muster romantic feelings for Norman again. As it turned out, the two-month separation was just what we really needed.

Norman flew up every weekend, and we'd go out on dates. After going to dinner, we'd go for long walks. We talked for hours and hours, and then he'd have to leave.

I called my mum to tell her what was happening. I ended the conversation by saying, "You know, I wonder if the feelings will ever come back. I wonder if we'll just develop a friendship—maybe that's all we'll have. Maybe we'll just be good friends, but we'll be the kind of good friends who will last for a lifetime." With her usual wisdom, Mum made little comment. She just kept praying.

The Hole in My Heart Finally Mended

I just couldn't imagine everything's being restored completely. Nonetheless, my love for Norman was gradually being rekindled, almost without my realizing it. It was during this time that I asked Norman to forgive me for all the things I had said to hurt him, because I wanted so much to see if he cared.

I realized that when I had married Norman, I had vowed unconsciously never to give myself completely to him, because that would just be too risky. I knew that after my dad died there was a hole in my heart, which I'd tried to fill with service to God and other things. But no matter what I tried to put in that hole, there were jagged edges in my soul and nothing would fit. I'd even tried to force Norman in there and make him help fill the void. But how could he have filled it when I didn't want to give myself fully to him? I guess we both realized that only Jesus can fill that void; only He can fill our hearts to overflowing.

I also realized that Norman had been just like me. He had been wounded when he was young. He had his fears and insecurities. He really wasn't an impenetrable wall that stood there waiting to knock me down. He was just as vulnerable as I was.

I Began to Look Forward to Friday

Falling back in love with Norman sort of crept up on me. The first couple of times he flew up to see me I'd go out to meet him and think, *I'm doing this because I have to*. But as the weeks went by, I'd find myself really missing Norman by Wednesday or Thursday. I began looking forward to Friday, when he would arrive. That took me by surprise. I was taken by surprise all along the line when my feelings for Norman returned so quickly.

After being in town about six weeks, I finally found an apartment to rent, and by the end of November Norman had finished his business in Nashville and was able to move in. Because most of our stuff was still in California, I rented all the furniture, and on the day he arrived I included one other touch.

I went out and bought several helium-filled balloons, half of which were printed with I LOVE YOU, and the other half with WELCOME HOME. I didn't want Norman to think he was coming back to live on some kind of trial basis. I wanted him to know that he was coming home and that I really loved him.

Balloons were all over the place—two in the bedroom, a big one on the front door, a couple in the lounge, a couple in the living room, a couple in the kitchen, and one in the bathroom. I could tell Norman was surprised. He kidded me about not being able to move around in the apartment because of all the balloons, but I knew he liked them.

Norman's homecoming proved to me that I had come to the place where I was able to let go. Before, I'd either wanted to possess Norman completely, or else I wanted nothing to do with him. Now we could begin a whole new life of loving each other, but not depending on each other for every single emotion and every good feeling.

I saw now that love wasn't something that would hurt

you. Before I had believed love was a scary thing because it made you vulnerable. Now I saw how love could make you stronger. My mum was not less of a person because my dad died. Instead, she became a much stronger person.

My mum reminds me of something Malcolm Muggeridge once said, to the effect that everything of worth that he had ever learned in over seventy years of life had been learned in adversity. Now I had a better grasp of how God often uses adversity to produce "perseverance; perseverance, character; and character, hope" (Rom. 5:3–4 NIV).

Maybe there would be a time when Norman would be taken from me or I would be taken from him, but God was now bigger than my fears. It was almost as if God slowly unpried my fingers and kept telling me gently, "Look, it's really okay because whatever happens, I'll be there. You have kept your covenant with Me, and I'll always keep My covenant with you."

Christmas Made Me Cry—with Joy

Christmas came, and in direct contrast to the Christmases of the past two years, this one was absolutely beautiful in every way. Norman wouldn't even give me a tiny hint about what he was giving me. Usually he was the one who wanted hints from me. He'd say, "I'm terrible at finding things for you. Tell me what you want, and I'll get it for you."

This time, however, he hadn't said a word, and I thought that was strange.

We woke up on Christmas morning, and he gave me my gift: a tiny box carefully wrapped in gold paper. I opened it, and there was a beautiful new wedding band. He took off my old band and put on the new one, saying, "I want you to know that I love you and that I am committed to you for the rest of our lives. I want this ring to be a symbol of our new beginning."

It was all so beautiful that it made me cry. Yes, the ring was beautiful, but something else was even more important—the love in Norman's eyes.

The next week was New Year's, and we had to fly to California because I was doing a big Youth for Christ benefit banquet in Orange County. At our table that New Year's Eve was an unusual couple. He was in a wheelchair, and she was on crutches. They spent most of the evening telling us their unusual love story—of how they had met and married and how neither of them wanted to marry a person who had a disability. Each had wanted somebody who was glamorous and "whole"; yet, they had learned what love really is.

I'll never forget the last minute of 1988. I had finished singing my last song and was sitting at the table with Norman. There was a huge clock on the wall, the largest clock I had ever seen in my life. All the lights were out, and only the candles on our tables illuminated the scene. Everyone sat in silence as the final sixty seconds of 1988 became history.

Never before had saying good-bye to the old meant so much. Good-bye to the pain, the heartache, the fear, the struggle, and all of the hurt and anger. It was all vanishing away in the last minute of a year that had seen us go through so much. Now a new year beckoned with a promise of something infinitely better because God was right in the middle of it.

I didn't look at Norman; I just watched the clock. I watched as every single second ticked away. When it struck midnight, Norman took me in his arms, kissed me, and said, "Happy New Year." I smiled and knew it would be more than that. It would be a happy new life together.

Epilogue

It has been well over a year since I fell back in love with my husband. Often I pause during the frantic rush of another day at the "700 Club" to thank God for him, for Kauai, and for a novel on spiritual warfare, which became an unlikely catalyst that helped me to pull together my tangled feelings and gave me the courage to persevere instead of giving up.

The other day, I came across something I wrote when Norman and I were going through our most difficult time. I'm no poet, but I love to try my hand at penning a few words now and then. Out of my pain and disillusionment with marriage, I wrote three stanzas and then stopped because I didn't know what else to say:

> You brought me the moon on a sailboat
> You scattered the stars at my door
> You swept me away from the black and the gray
> To an island we slept on the shore.
>
> They told us we'd never survive, my friend,
> They gave us a year and a day
> For no one has life on a fool's paradise.
> At midnight, the boat slips away.
>
> And, Oh, how I wished that the dreaming was true
> And, Oh, how I cried when I knew
> That the fairy tale lies in my rose-colored eyes
> Wouldn't make it for me and for you.

Rereading those sad lines reminded me of something I had read recently about how real love comes in three stages. First, there is initial romance and infatuation, the red roses, the dinner dates, being met at the train with your heart thumping. Next, there seems to come a time of disillusionment, when you realize that for all dreams "there is a morning after." The things that once held you to each other appear to be threads that are too thin to last a lifetime. But, finally, you can come to a third stage. If you can hold on, you discover a rare treasure that is worth all of the pain and the struggle.

I had found my treasure, and I knew it was time to add a final verse:

> But you stood by my side, like a true friend
> You shed a few tears with me, too
> And the love that we share
> Never dreamt it was there,
> Is the anchor that our hearts cling to.

SEVEN

Keeping It Simple
Keeps It Real

*When this complex, plastic world tries to squeeze us into
a designer mold, we can let fear and pride
take over, or we can shake free to live the simple
truth of the gospel with humility and love.*

It happened on the freeway, just a few weeks after I started cohosting the "700 Club." I suppose you could say my integrity got slapped in the face, and to tell the truth, I needed it!

Ever since my decision on the beach at Kauai, I wanted to walk more closely with God than ever. I wanted no more hiding, no more pretense.

I wanted to be real, not plastic in any way. Maybe that's why I was especially tuned in one evening as I drove back to the hotel after another long day of broadcasts, tapings, and phone calls.

I flipped on the radio, hoping for a little lift from one of the local Christian stations, and a familiar song filled the car. The vocalist was someone I knew well in the Christian music industry. There had been a day when that song would have given me what I was looking for. I used to play it while doing housework and, instead of feeling drowned in drudgery, I'd wind up having a ball. But on this particular evening, the song didn't do a thing for me.

The lyrics didn't come close to what I was feeling and where I was hurting, especially for other people. After being on the "700 Club" for just a few weeks, I had new sensitivity to what was happening in the world and how badly people needed a healing touch from Christ.

My Friends Told Me I Was Selling Out

When I told my friends that I was praying about Pat Robertson's invitation to become cohost for the "700 Club," some of them told me, "If you take that job, you'll bury your head in Christian television, and you'll never breathe clean air again. You'll wind up sheltering yourself from the real world. You're selling out to the 'Blue Rinse Brigade'!"

But a funny thing had happened to me on my way to irrelevancy. From the very first week, cohosting the "700 Club" broadcasts was like having God throw a bucket of ice water in my face every morning. I realized that, while I had thought I knew about needs and hurts, I didn't really know much at all.

I'd given plenty of Christian concerts and even counseled people afterward, but now it seemed that I had been singing happy little Christian songs for nice Christian people. We'd all have fun and then go home feeling, "Wow! We've really met some needs tonight."

I'm sure we did meet some needs, but now I became aware of so many more. Daily I was dealing with people who had been brought up in desperate poverty, people caught in the trap of prostitution, drug addiction, child abuse, and a myriad of other human tragedies.

I had been so busy during those first few weeks that I hadn't realized how much I was changing. Now, one song on the radio brought it all home. I actually pulled the car off on an emergency parking space and sat there thinking, *What on earth have I been doing all this time? All these people are out there with real, open wounds, and so much of what I did was like blowing up balloons and saying, "Yippee! Let's all love Jesus!"*

"I'm Tired of Being a Hamster"

Later, I told Norman what had happened and concluded by saying, "I'm not even sure I want to make another album. I don't want to be a hamster on a treadmill. Every year I turn out an album, and I do a tour because it's expected. If what I sing really doesn't make a difference, I'm not sure I want to do anymore."

Norman understood how I felt, and he urged me to get in touch with Dan Posthuma, who was head of the Myrrh label at Word Records, the division that recorded my albums. "That's a good idea," I agreed. By the next day, however, I was caught up in the intense routine at the "700 Club," and I forgot about making the call.

Less than ten days later, however, Dan Posthuma called me: "Sheila, it's about that time again. What's your thinking for a new album?"

I shared with Dan what had happened to me, and then I added, "You know, Dan, I'm not sure I want to do another album. I don't know where I am anymore in this whole thing."

Instead of getting angry or pressuring me to produce another product, Dan said, "I understand. Why don't we get together and talk about this? Greg Nelson has expressed some interest in doing something."

Greg Nelson is one of the top producers in the country and has done albums for people like Sandy Patti and Steve Green. I flew down to Nashville to talk with Greg. I told him what had been going on with me. As I shared my story with him, his eyes filled with tears. "Sheila," he said, "I agree with you with all my heart. I don't want to just turn out another record. I want to make a difference."

We decided to get together for a brainstorming weekend—Dan, Greg, Norman, Steve Lorenz,[1] and I. We chose Dallas, somewhat of a midway point for all of us.

I prepared for that weekend by writing down the subjects that I had been thinking about a great deal recently. I wanted to sing about what it's like to be alone, what it's like to be disillusioned, and to have all your dreams crumble around you. Was there any good news I could bring to people? Was there anything I could take to the streets, to the living rooms, to the concert stage that would make sense the way Jesus made sense when He spoke to His listeners' deepest needs?

We checked in at the hotel in Dallas and had a weekend-long "listening party." Whenever you are thinking about doing a new album, you put out the word, and songwriters send in their latest efforts. Dan brought some great new songs that had come in for his consideration, and Greg brought others as well. We had dozens of songs to sort out as we listened, talked, and prayed. As the hours went by, we identified the things we thought were important. We were looking for a plumb line—ten issues or subjects that would communicate the truth of the gospel.

Over that weekend, we heard many really great songs. We knew that a lot of them would get plenty of air play, but if they didn't say what we wanted the album to say, we declined to do them. Every song had to speak the simple truth, the kind of truth that touches your soul and takes root in your heart. In the words of William Yeats, the English poet:

> God guard me from those thoughts men think in the mind alone;
> He that sings a lasting song, thinks in marrow bone.

We wanted every one of these songs to be a lasting one, something that would communicate the Word of God, which the writer of Hebrews says is living and active and sharper than any two-edged sword.[2]

It was a tough weekend because we had to balance our need to be artistic, creative, and poetic with what we felt was more important—the need to be real, helpful, and true to the simple truth of the gospel. We had to decide how much we valued our integrity as musicians and entertainers against how much we valued our integrity as servants of Christ.

From Sand to Solid Rock

For my *Shadow Lands* album, which had come out several years before, I had recorded several songs that spoke of Christ, but in the commercial pop rock vein. The album was fairly successful, and it got great reviews in many different Christian magazines, which said I was on the "radical cutting edge of Christian rock music."

Typical of the songs in the album was "Sand in the Hand," which included these lyrics:

> Love is a miracle, a vision to see
> Sand in the hand will run away
> But love in the heart will stay
> Sand in the hand will run away, run away.
> It's not just a dream, love is forevermore and ever
>   green.[3]

Not exactly *War and Peace*, but the kind of stuff that kids love to repeat without doing much thinking.

For our new album, however, we wrote songs like "When You Come into His Kingdom." A few lines of that song show the difference:

Another morning comes, you give yourself away
To a million things that take your time
You lose another day.
Your dreams can fall apart and cry out in despair
You built your world so carefully and no one seems to
    care.
But there's a place for travel-worn and weary ones
You can leave your dusty shoes outside the door.
For when you come into His Kingdom
You're going to find love
Find that you've just begun
When you come into His Kingdom, no matter who, no
    matter what you've done.[1]

We Settled on *Simple Truth*

The result of our weekend together was an album, appropriately titled *Simple Truth*. Its ten songs spoke of God's calling of love, losing your life so you can find it, being there for others, quiet times with God, and giving Him all the glory. We even included the old hymn "Savior, Like a Shepherd Lead Us," because it so clearly stated the simple walk of the committed Christian.

The first time I performed songs from *Simple Truth* in concert was at the Billy Graham Crusade in London in 1989, which was broadcast by satellite across Great Britain. A few days later, I received a letter from a woman in northern England, whose brother had attended the meeting and heard me sing "God Loves You." A medical doctor, he had never been particularly interested in the claims of the gospel before, but as he heard the words of the song he felt God's presence in a new and different way and realized for the very first time that God did love him. Even before Dr. Graham preached, this man had made up his mind from hearing my song. He went forward and gave his life to Christ.

Another letter, from a young woman who had had an

abortion, told me of how she had been a Christian, but life had closed in upon her. She thought she had no choice but to kill the child in her womb, and she had lived in a nightmare of guilt ever since. She bought *Simple Truth,* and when she heard "God Loves You," she realized that God had forgiven her and that she could at last forgive herself.

Letters like these are far more meaningful to me than favorable reviews, lots of air play, or even big sales. *Simple Truth* was our team effort to do away with plastic, designer-suit Christianity and go for the real thing. Ever since the televangelist scandals broke in headlines and over TV newscasts, Christian integrity has been under greater scrutiny and criticism than ever. I clearly remember where I was and what I was doing when the sad news of Jim Bakker's private life hit the headlines.

It Was Like a Soap Opera, but Worse

I had crawled out of bed and was having some breakfast when I flipped on the news, to be greeted with a report that stunned me. I knew Jim and Tammy Bakker and had made several appearances on their PTL show. Disbelief washed across me in huge waves as I heard the lurid details that sounded like a soap opera out of control. The ill-disguised delight on the face of the cynical TV reporter was a sign of what was to come in media coverage during the following weeks and months. One more evangelical figurehead was being toppled, and I could tell this reporter was relishing his work.

I needed to get out into the fresh air, to think and pray. I felt bombarded by mixed emotions: anger, sorrow, disappointment, but most of all, sadness.

I found myself outside a favorite little French café a few blocks from where we were living in Laguna Beach. As I sat on the patio with the steam of cappuccino competing with the heat of the day, I began to write the lyrics to a song on a table napkin with a borrowed pencil.

Up until then, I had done little or no writing of my own songs. But for some reason, that morning it seemed easy for me to express my heart, and the words to "It Could Have Been Me" flowed out. Another fragile Christian warrior had indeed slipped. He had fallen from grace, and now the vultures were circling.

So much of our Christian heritage seems to be built on a pyramid system. The person at the top has a long way to fall, and many delight in kicking him or her on the way down.

Why are we so cruel to each other? Why do we hit out so violently when someone crumbles? I'm not saying that sin should not be dealt with—far from it. I believe with all my heart in discipline within the body of Christ. I guess I'm referring to the spectators who cheer as the blade falls, who find it so much easier to believe the worst than to hold onto the best. Perhaps we hit out most strongly at those who live out our private temptations. As I said in "It Could Have Been Me,"

> And in our hearts we fear
> The ones whose lives are like our own
> Whose shadows dance like demons in our minds.[5]

Two ideas motivated me as I put down the words for the song on that napkin. Already I was looking ahead to the months of endless headlines and "news angles." I could picture the ridicule and scorn that would be heaped upon the church as a whole, for surely this kind of tragedy would be a late night talk show host's dream.

But even more important, as I thought of Jim and Tammy Bakker fielding reporters' cynical questions, I realized that in many ways it could have been me. Long before the PTL

It Could Have Been Me

I heard the news today that another soldier stumbled,
A fragile warrior slipped and fell from grace.
The vultures swooped to tear his heart
And pin him to the ground
And from the shadows someone took his place.

Today we'll talk amongst ourselves,
We never bought his words.
We'll say we saw the madness in his eye.
Tomorrow he's forgotten as we've scrubbed him from our hearts
And as he bleeds we slowly turn our eyes.

But it could have been me.
I could have been the one to lose my grip and fall.
It could have been me,
The one who takes pride in always standing tall.
For unless you hold me tightly, Lord, and I can hold on, too,
Then tomorrow in the news it could be me.

And in our hearts we fear the ones whose lives are like our own,
Whose shadows dance like demons in our minds.
We think to push them far away
We'll exorcise our souls.
We'll make them play the tune for all mankind.

But it could have been me.
I could have been the one to lose my grip and fall.
It could have been me,
The one who takes pride in always standing tall.
For unless you hold me tightly, Lord, and I can hold on, too,
Then tomorrow in the news it could be me.[6]

scandal broke, the Lord had been gently dealing with my overconfidence. I had always felt strong as a Christian, that with Jesus by my side I could go anywhere, do anything, withstand any pressure and temptation. I never realized the subtle trap of my naïve pride.

Just as James and John asked Jesus if they could sit on His right and left in heaven, so also I wanted to be right up there with them. When the Lord asked whether they knew what they were saying, like pompous children they declared their suitability for the job. But history bears out that they were not able to stand when Jesus stood, not able to bleed when He bled. Only He is able. We never have been; we never will be. If we are truthful with ourselves, we must reject pride and self-reliance and admit that we are not able to stand without Jesus.

Without God's grace in our lives, then, truly it could be us. Our daily choices can make us or break us. This complex, plastic world can squeeze us into its designer mold, or we can strive to live the simple truths of the gospel with humility and love.

I remember attending a convention at which Luis Palau, the Argentinean evangelist, was the main speaker. His theme was the well-known challenge from Jesus to "take up your cross and follow Me."[7] As Palau held that challenge before us, we were faced with our lack of understanding. We like to cradle spiritual phrases, clutching them to our bosoms, but they are useless if there is no daily application in our lives.

Each day we have to make choices. Often, they are not choices between extremes of good and evil where the answer is apparent. The answer seems to lie somewhere in the gray, and that is where we can quickly become tarnished.

When Satan Is Most Dangerous

Working in a medium like television leaves you highly visible—and very vulnerable. Weekly I learn that walking as Christ walked requires delicate balance. I meet many people who are asking, "Where are You, God? Are You really there, or is my faith just something I've built to form a crutch?" For many people, Satan is definitely there, perched on their backs, creating havoc and chaos of all kinds.

Satan can be subtle, and he's never more dangerous than when you think you've made some progress as a Christian, that you've done something right and you "just know God is pleased." Since we all have the clay feet of fallibility, it's important for us to have a healthy assessment of our weaknesses as well as our strengths. If we don't, we can wind up taking our eyes off Jesus and find ourselves in the mud. As I began working on this book, I learned again that Christian living isn't putting notches on your spiritual gun; it's walking the way of the pilgrim. Sometimes you move forward at a good pace, and other times you make choices that force you to slip back.

Cindy Was Dying of Leukemia

It was early November and well past 6:00 in the evening. It had been a long day, during which I had taped four shows for "Heart to Heart." I was looking forward to a rare weekend at home—no traveling, no concerts, just kicking back with Norman to relax.

I was at my desk, picking up a few things for Monday's "700 Club," when Laura, my secretary, stopped me.

"Sheila, we just got a call from one of our Founder members. He's a doctor in a children's hospital in Phoenix."

"Did he say what he wanted?" I asked, glancing at my watch.

"He has a young patient, a fourteen-year-old girl who is dying of leukemia. You're her favorite singer. She has your tape by her bed and listens to it all the time. She'd really like you to call."

"Do you have the hospital's number and the girl's name?"

Laura give me the slip of paper, and as I looked at the name Cindy and the number, weariness flooded over me as I thought of what I might say to a dying girl when I was feeling so tired myself.

I looked at Laura, hoping she could see how weary I was and then said, "Maybe it could wait until Monday?"

Laura didn't say anything, but her raised eyebrows sent me a signal. I put the slip of paper in my purse and headed for the elevator. As I punched the button, I knew I had made the wrong decision. I turned around and hurried past Laura, saying, "I'm just going to go ahead and call this girl. I really think I should."

As I dialed the number, I asked God for help—and a lot of wisdom. What do you say to a fourteen-year-old girl who's dying? How do you comfort someone whose life force is being sucked away?

The call went through, and a tired voice answered, "Hello, can I help you?"

I swallowed quickly, "Yes, this is Sheila Walsh. I'm calling about Cindy."

"Oh, Sheila, I'm *so* glad you called. I'm Cindy's mother."

She told me how weak her daughter was and then went on; "She won't be able to talk. She's in a lot of pain. Please don't be distressed by her little moans. She really loves you, and she'll be so happy to hear your voice. I'm going to hold the phone to her ear."

Lord, help me, please. What do I say?

"Hi, Cindy, it's Sheila. I'm so sorry you're sick."

I talked for a while, telling Cindy that the Lord loved her

140

and that I was praying for her. All I could hear were little sounds, almost like a tiny animal in distress. Then I began to read from a few of my favorite psalms, beginning with Psalm 91: "He who dwells in the shelter of the Most High will rest in the shadow of the Almighty. . . . Surely He will save you from the fowler's snare and from the deadly pestilence" (NIV).

Next I turned to Psalm 139: "O LORD, you have searched me and you know me. . . . you have laid your hand upon me. . . . your hand will guide me, your right hand will hold me fast" (NIV).

And finally I read from Psalm 23, the familiar words taking on a new and poignant meaning at that moment: "The LORD is my shepherd, I shall lack nothing. . . . Even though I walk through the valley of the shadow of death, I will fear no evil, for you are with me; . . . Surely goodness and love will follow me . . . and I will dwell in the house of the LORD forever" (NIV).

I prayed with Cindy, and then her mom came back on the line: "Sheila, she's smiling. Thank you." I gave Cindy's mother my home phone number and told her to feel free to call me.

When I came back in on Monday morning, there was a message. Cindy was with the Lord. I sat at my desk and wept for her family. I felt so sad for the painful weeks and months that lay ahead: their first Christmas without her, her birthday, her friends growing into womanhood. For Cindy, there was no more pain. For those left behind, there would be many hard days.

"Thank You, Lord. Oh, thank You so much," I said as I allowed myself to think for a moment about how I would have felt if I hadn't called.

In a few days I received a lovely letter from Cindy's doctor, who told me how much it had meant to Cindy and her mother that I had called. Cindy had attended my concert in Phoenix the year before. There had been no sign of leukemia then, but when it struck it had worked very rapidly to destroy her body.

Helping Cindy as she stood on the threshold of heaven was hard, but in a strange and wonderful way it was also good. It was one of those times I was sure I had been obedient to what God was telling me. As I lay in bed that night, I thought about how I had changed from being a presumptuous teenager who wanted God to give her all of Scotland. "Lord," I prayed, "I don't want to talk so much about great exploits. I just want to try to live them in small ways."

I fell asleep feeling good because I had done what God told me to do when He told me to do it, which is always a good idea. I forgot for a moment that I still had clay feet, but as I slept, it began to rain.

How Clay Feet Can Slip in a Hurry

Three weeks after I talked to Cindy, I found myself working late at the office again, this time on the night before the first Thanksgiving Norman and I would have in our new townhouse.

"Why do you want lamb for Thanksgiving?" I asked him that morning. "This is America, for goodness sake, we're talking turkey. You know, a big, round, fat bird."

"You asked me what I wanted," Norman had indignantly replied. "And I want lamb—roast leg of lamb. I want mint jelly and roast potatoes, peas and carrots, but most of all I want a nice juicy lamb."

I finished up my work for the day and looked at my watch. It was 5:30, and I told myself, "Okay, you're out of here."

I grabbed my car keys and was headed for the door when Laura's familiar voice stopped me: "Sheila!"

As I turned, Laura said, "We've had a call from a young girl. Her name is Jennifer. She's eighteen, and she says she really needs to talk with you. I think she's in real trouble."

Oh, great! I muttered to myself. *She thinks she's in trouble! If I don't get out of here, I'll never find that leg of lamb for tomorrow's dinner.*

"Do you think I could wait for a couple of days before I call her?" I asked Laura.

"No, I really don't," Laura said. "The girl mentioned something about suicide."

I grabbed the slip of paper and with mixed emotions headed down to my dressing room to make the call. One part of me was screaming, *You've got to get out of here. You're already late, and you've got stops to make on the way home.*

But another voice said, *If you don't call, it's going to ruin your Thanksgiving, and you're not going to enjoy that lamb. You'll feel guilty because you didn't make the call.*

I dialed the number, and as I waited for the connection, I struggled out of my shirt and skirt and tried to get into my jeans.

"Hello," said a very quiet voice.

"Hi, Jennifer? This is Sheila Walsh. I hear you wanted to talk to me."

I kicked my shoes into the closet and tried to reach for my sneakers, almost pulling the phone off the wall.

"Oh, thanks for calling. I didn't think you'd call."

"Well, yeah, Jennifer, of course I'd call you. I care. That's why I called you."

I knew those were the right words to say, but I didn't really feel them deep in my heart at that moment. Jennifer began talking about her life, which she thought was very unfair. It didn't take her long to start making statements that sounded unfair to everyone else as well. She had no friends, and nobody cared for her at all. No, she didn't go to church

143

because nobody in any of the churches really loved her; besides, she loved God more than anybody else anyhow.

Jennifer went on like this for several minutes, and I began to get irritated. "How can you say you love God more than anybody?" I said a bit crossly. "If you really loved God, it would make you more loving rather than just feeling sorry for yourself."

I was hoping that being a bit firm with Jennifer would help. At least that's what I told myself, but what I was really saying was, "Hurry up and get better fast, because I've got to go out and buy this jolly leg of lamb and be ready for Thanksgiving."

Then I heard her say, "You know, I just called up to get you to pray for me." And she proceeded to quote the verse that we're always quoting on the "700 Club": "I tell you that if two of you on earth agree about something, then you can pray for it. And the thing you ask for will be done for you by my Father in heaven" (Matt. 18:19).

"But, Jennifer, I'm not sure I can pray," I told her. "We can't pray together because we don't agree. You tell me you love God but that you've decided to take your own life. You're telling me you can look at the cross and literally say to Jesus, 'Hey, You blew it. I'm not worth what You did when You died for me.' You're telling Jesus that He was wrong and that your only way out is to end it."

"Well," said Jennifer after a few seconds of silence, "I've got bulimia, and I'm going to die anyway, so what's the difference?"

I asked her to tell me about it, and her story poured out. Over the past three years, she had thrown up every day of her life. Her symptoms sounded like those of a true bulimic, straight down the line. Because of all her vomiting, the enamel on her teeth had dissolved. I was convinced that she was truly in a bad way. I also started feeling convicted about getting too firm with her.

144

We had talked for over twenty minutes when she said, "I'm going to have to go now because I'm meeting my mom, and if I'm late she'll get really angry. Everybody in my family gets angry. All there is in our house is anger. I didn't call wanting you to get angry with me. Why are you angry with me? I thought you would pray for me. I just need a friend. I should have known you were just like everybody else."

I became a bit irritated and protested, "Jennifer, I wouldn't have called if I were just like everybody else. . . ."

My words were barely out of my mouth when I realized that Jennifer was right. I sat for a few moments in stunned silence, exposed, ugly, a fraud. I *had* been acting like everybody else. I had really blown it—big time blown it. Jennifer had been holding onto heaven with hell on her back, but she was ready to let go of everything, and I wasn't helping her much.

"Look, Jennifer, I'm really sorry. I know you're right. I have no right to get angry with you, and I'm really sorry. Do you still want me to pray for you?"

There was more silence, and then Jennifer finally said, "Yeah. . . . I really would love for you to pray for me. I'm all alone."

After I prayed for Jennifer and we were saying our good-byes, she said, "I'd love it if I could just call sometimes. I just want to know there is another way to live, and I know you're right. I know there's another way to live, but I just can't find it. I just can't get out of myself right now."

I Wasn't Mother Teresa After All

We hung up, and I got down on my knees and wept, sliding in the muddy mess my clay feet had left. I saw myself so clearly, and I asked God to forgive me for the anger and pride that made me try to fit Jennifer into a slot. To me, she had been problem "3A." I knew the solution to problem

"3A," but Jennifer just wouldn't fit. She just wouldn't grab my pat answers quickly enough to let me get out there, to do all the things I had to do.

Talking to Jennifer slapped me in the face with my own humanity. I realized I hadn't become Mother Teresa overnight after all. I wanted to be the kind of person who could be there for people, but I knew that I was human just like everyone else. I'm not just "Sheila who's always waiting at the other end of the line at the '700 Club.'" I have a home and a husband, and that night I wanted to get home and fix him the best Thanksgiving dinner he had ever had.

Sometimes the most loving thing God can do is to hold up a mirror before our faces and let us gaze at the stark reality of what we're really like. I hadn't been honest enough to say, "Laura, I'm tired, and I have several things to do before I go home. Can you get one of our phone counselors involved?" I guess I was afraid I would damage my good name as a "caring" person.

Neither had I been honest enough to say, "Lord, I don't want to make this call. I want to go home, but someone needs my help, so I need Yours. Please give me Your love and help me to communicate it."

I had forgotten to pray. I had been in a hurry, and I thought I could handle this caller in just a few minutes and be on my way. I learned a good lesson that day. One of the keys to holding onto heaven is to have healthy humility and to be ever aware of the dangers of subtle pride.

The minute we begin to believe our own publicity, we are in for a nasty slide. The moment we feel we are invincible, the enemy crawls through one of the cracks of our pride and delights in showing us otherwise. Pride can be so subtle. It always begins with lies—the little comforting lies that we tell ourselves: "You're not like everybody else. You're strong. It'll never happen to you."

The truth is that we are all flawed creatures, and if we crawl out from under the protective wing of the Lord, we are most vulnerable. As Joy Dawson said, "There are no extraordinary Christians. Only ordinary Christians who serve an extraordinary God."

As Christ built His church, He picked very ordinary people to be His disciples, and there was no better example of how ordinary a follower of Christ could be than Peter. When it came to clay feet, he wore size twelve and then some.

"Lord, I'll Never Fail You!"

Peter made the same mistake I had made. He bought into Satan's lie: "You're not like everybody else. You're strong. It'll never happen to you." We know the scene well. After eating their Passover supper, Jesus and His disciples were preparing to leave for the Mount of Olives, but Jesus paused to tell them, "Tonight you will lose your faith because of Me." Then He quoted from the prophet Zechariah, saying, "I will kill the shepherd and the sheep will scatter" (Zech. 13:7).

Peter, however, protested. He knew the Lord couldn't be referring to him! He interrupted Jesus, saying, "All the others may lose their faith, but I will never lose mine!"

Jesus fixed him with a knowing look: "Peter, I tell you the truth. Before the night is out, you will deny Me three times."

"Not so, Lord!" responded Peter. "I'll never do that. I'll even die with You!" And then the Gospel account adds an interesting sentence: "And all the other followers said the same thing."[8]

Three hours later, Peter denied Christ. Not once. Not twice. But three times, just as Jesus had predicted.

Peter was no different from any of us. He needed the Lord's protective wing. There are no extraordinary Christians, even in the Bible. We all have feet of clay. We all falter when we succumb to the sin of pride.

Despite Peter's failures, Jesus gave him another chance, just as He does for you and me.

After the Resurrection, Jesus and Peter met face-to-face on the shores of the Sea of Galilee to take care of unfinished business. Jesus did not plan to humiliate Peter, but He did want him to know the difference between the humble trust that was now in his heart and the foolish pride that he had displayed the night before the Crucifixion.

Three times Jesus asked the same question: "Peter, do you love Me? Yes, I known you've blown it, and I know you're ashamed, but that's not what I'm asking, Peter. I want to know, do you love Me?"

Peter looked into the eyes of the Son of God, his guilt bathed in the sea of Jesus' overwhelming love, and said, "Lord, You know everything. You know that I love You!"

And the Lord answered, "Then take care of My sheep."[9]

When Peter heard his assignment from the Lord, he knew beyond any doubt that he had been forgiven. Now he was ready to walk closely in His Master's footsteps because he had a new understanding of why and how his feet were made of clay.

So it is with all of us. We're going to make mistakes. We do fall flat on our faces at times. We are fallible and flawed, but Christ is able and willing to restore us. If we love Him, if we truly love Him, He will save us from our pride.

The Lord used Jennifer to remind me of what can happen when I try to stand on my own two clay feet without His help. When the stormy days come with all their pressures, it's going to be a mess, and everybody is going to get covered with mud.

I was also reminded that the Christian's direction is always forward, but there are bound to be detours and some slipping back. Sometimes you think you've become something special, because God has given you grace enough to be there for some people and to see them helped, as Cindy was helped. And then, just as you begin to go off on a tangent and become satisfied with how incredible you are and how willing you are just to be there for everybody, you are suddenly brought up short. You realize that you're still selfish, and a leg of lamb can become more important than an eighteen-year-old who thinks she has nothing to live for.

Pride is insidious. It can do its worst harm at moments when we think we're the most humble, the most misunderstood, the most "righteous." Even Job had to find that out.

Job Couldn't See Past His Self-righteousness

After refuting the arguments of three friends who had come to set him straight, Job made a speech that turned into a long list of his spiritual accomplishments. As he ended his speech, Job said,

> Now let God All-Powerful answer me.
>   Let the one who is against me write
>   down what he accuses me of.
> I would surely wear the writing on my
>   shoulder.
>   I would put it on like a crown.
> I would explain to God every step I took.
>   I would come near to God like a prince.
> (Job 31:35–37)

Blinded by his pain, Job was now having trouble seeing past his self-righteousness. So God sent someone to set Job straight.

Elihu had been standing among the crowd that was listening to the debate between Job and the three older men who were supposed to have special wisdom born of many years of experience. He apologized for his youth, but he knew he had a word for Job straight from God. He told Job that his claims of being pure and without sin, innocent, and free from all guilt were wrong because no one can say that.[10]

Elihu proclaimed God's sovereignty, pointing out that God sometimes speaks one way and sometimes another and that people don't always understand. God warns us not to be proud in order to save our souls from death.[11] God All-Powerful never does wrong, never twists what is right.[12]

Elihu's speech went on and on, punctuated several times by invitations to Job to speak up or to maintain silence if he had nothing to say and wanted to learn wisdom. Significantly, Job *never* interrupted Elihu. He had countered the arguments of the other three men time and time again, but Elihu said his piece and Job listened because Job knew that Elihu spoke the truth.

Job had been made aware of his clay feet. He was ready to accept whatever came from God's hand. He had learned the secret of humility.

I'm still learning the secret and that's what helps keep my life simple.

EIGHT

God Has Left Us
a Job to Do

When the needy cross our path,
we can choose to show selfish indifference,
or we can take our eyes off our own needs
and follow Jesus to love the unlovely.

It was hot and sticky. The air was filled with dust as we landed in Manila in January 1988 to film a TV documentary about the work of Compassion International, a Christian child sponsorship agency. I had worked with Compassion for almost six years. From Los Angeles to New York, I would often speak in my concerts about the difference Compassion makes in the lives of the children who are born with so little.

I knew all the statistics. Three out of every five children are born in Third World nations, and one in three of those will die before they are five years old due to the ravages of malnutrition and disease. While we spend millions on the latest diet craze, children die for lack of a piece of bread.

Now Compassion had invited me to help bring the enormity of the problem to the people back in the United States. I was more than willing to be involved in helping God's people understand our opportunity to reach out to those whose silent screams break the Father's heart.

As we left the air terminal, an incredible scene assaulted our senses. I've never seen so many people in one place at one time, all moving, all pushing, all going in different directions. I was falling over children and chickens at the same time, trying not to scratch the several mosquito bites I had suffered in the past three minutes. The Philippine gentleman who came to pick us up grinned from ear to ear.

"I think it will take us some time to get out of here, yes?"

I agreed, but I didn't care because I was having too much fun. As I stood on the roof of a truck to take photos of the heaving masses, I felt like Indiana Walsh in "Raiders of the Lost Airport."

Our friends in the film crew had already arrived and were hard at work. We spent the first couple of days visiting various Compassion projects—schools, villages, new wells, and water pumps.

On the third morning we made an early start because the school we were due to film was some distance away. I got up at 5:00 A.M. to shower, and as I did my makeup for the cameras, I thought, *This is all a bit pointless. In this heat I'm just going to melt, drip, and run anyway.*

By 7:00 A.M. we were all in the jeep and heading out across the dusty roads. We arrived a little before nine and wandered in to watch the classes in progress. The little school had begun with one teacher and two or three children, but through the prayers and hard work of the local people and the support of Compassion, it had grown significantly.

Each time the school grew too big for the building, they simply added another room. It was no architectural masterpiece, but it spoke of those who have a dream and never give up hope.

I sat with the class during its morning worship service and was amazed as each child recited a memory verse. Those children knew more of the Bible by heart in their eight short years than I had learned in thirty. Unexpectedly, the teacher announced that I was going to sing "Jesus Loves Me." As I sang the well-worn words, they took on a meaning I could never have imagined before coming to the Philippines.

When I came to the phrase "Little ones to Him belong, they are weak, but He is strong," I knew that I was looking right into the faces of some of those little ones God cared about so very much. I felt overwhelmed by a sense of God's compassion for each one.

Belinda Was One of Ten Children

One girl in particular caught my eye. She seemed shy, very quiet, very small. I asked the teacher about her and learned that her name was Belinda and that she had no sponsor. I knew that Norman would be 100 percent behind me, and so I said that we would love to be her sponsors.

As school broke up for the day and the children scattered outside, screaming and yelling, much like children anywhere, someone suggested that we might go and meet Belinda's family. We took a jeep as far as we could and then set off on foot, deeper and deeper into a kind of shanty town. The homes were built over a swamp, and the stench from the open sewers was almost unbearable.

Our Philippine interpreter went on ahead to explain to Belinda's mother who we were and why we were there, but I felt uncomfortable. How would this poor woman, who lived in a one-room shack with ten children, react to our uninvited invasion? A cameraman was with us, and I wondered, *Had we come to meet this woman or just to pump up our TV special?*

Nothing could have prepared me for the love that poured from that woman's heart toward me. She threw her arms around my neck and wept on my shoulder. I began weeping, too, and we clung together, total strangers, surrounded by her ten children crawling through the mud and chasing skinny chickens out of the room that was their kitchen, living room, and bedroom all in one. As I glanced over to the corner, I saw a cockroach crawling over the baby, and I wondered whether this little one would make it.

As we stood in the doorway, the mother told me through an interpreter the things that brought her joy and the things that broke her heart. I looked at her eight daughters, and I wondered what the future held for them. What kind of weddings would they have? What would they wear? Where would they live?

I looked into the woman's eyes and was surprised by her hope and courage. She told me that the Lord's presence fills her home, that His glory is with them. We prayed together as best we could with our mixed languages, and I turned to leave. As I walked away, tears blurred my vision, and I stepped off the plank right into the mud. I stopped to wipe the tears from my eyes, and as I looked down, there was Belinda's mother, on her knees in the mud, trying to wipe off my shoes as her children looked on with concern.

I couldn't speak. I could only give Belinda and her mom one more hug, and then I hurried away.

As we worked our way back to the jeep, one of the film crew members asked, "Are you all right, Sheila?"

"Yeah, I'll be okay if you just leave me alone for a few moments."

I wandered off across the field, my only companion a lethargic water buffalo. Manila was still hot, sticky, and dirty, but I would never be the same.

A Song Was Born in That Swamp

A few days later, as the wheels of our jetliner left the tarmac of Manila's airport, words from Jesus' well-known para-

154

ble kept running through my mind: *For I was hungry and you gave Me something to eat. I was thirsty, and you gave Me something to drink. . . . whatever you did for me of the least of these brothers of mine, you did for Me.*[1]

Already I was thinking about a song that would someday appear on one of my albums. When I got back to the States, I teamed with Rod Trott and Jon Sweet to do "Angels with Dirty Faces," which eventually became part of the album *Say So.* I admit that the lyrics take poetic license of sorts, but there is still an important message there. Scripture tells us that when we reach out to strangers, we might be entertaining angels without knowing it.[2] Who is to say? Perhaps we meet angels more often than we think. As the song puts it:

> This one is black
> This one is white
> This one is running away
> This one is you
> This one is me
> This one is dying to stay.
>
> Each one with our own unwritten story
> Comedy, tragedy, farce
> Looking for love on the road
> To glory at last.
>
> We're all angels with dirty faces
> Battered and bruised by the fall
> Angels with dirty faces, that's all.[3]

All of us are battered and bruised by the Fall. But when we care enough to reach out to one another in Jesus' Name, we all have a future and a hope.

Our Compassion Is Needed Everywhere

The Philippines have no corner on poverty and misery. You can find the poor, the desperate, and the unlovely on the back streets of any good-sized community in America or any other country of the world. Sometimes you can find them right on your own television screen.

I had just finished taping a special series of "Heart to Heart" programs at a celebrity mansion in Beverly Hills, California. We had filmed eleven "Heart to Heart" shows in three days, and I'd talked to an amazing assortment of inspiring people, including film stars Roy Rogers and Dale Evans, Rhonda Fleming, and Pat Boone. I had also interviewed Stormie Omartian, the beautiful singer/songwriter, and Al Kasha, the Academy-Award-winning composer.

My final taping had included two programs with Mario Murillo, who wrote a book called *Critical Mass: A Strategy for a North American Revival.* "Critical mass" is a nuclear term that refers to the minimum amount of radioactive material that can and will sustain a nuclear chain reaction. Mario believes that God is looking for another kind of critical mass—a core group of Christians who will be so sold out to Him with no ulterior motives that they will bring about revival.

As Mario talked with me, he described how at times, as he prays for people, an unbearable burden comes upon him. He has to continue to pray until it lifts.

After we wrapped up the interview and Mario had left, the rest of the shooting crew planned to have a celebration dinner, but I felt too tired to join them. I drove my rental car back to the hotel and sat there thinking about what Mario had said.

Never in my life had I prayed the way he had described. Never had I felt an unbearable burden where it would seem that God had shared His heart with me for a moment. I began asking the Lord if this was something He only shared with certain people who sought it and wouldn't take no for an answer.

I dialed room service, ordered a hamburger and cup of

coffee, and then turned on the television set. Geraldo Rivera's show was on. I'd never seen his program, but I had heard enough about his reputation for being sensational.

As I reached to switch channels, I noticed that his subject for the day was teenage prostitution. I decided to watch and see what he had to say.

His five guests were all young teenaged girls who had been prostitutes on the streets of New York. They had all chosen to leave the oldest profession, and they were on the program to tell Geraldo and millions of viewers what it had been like to sell themselves on the streets.

Four of the girls were rather blasé; but one talked lucidly about not being able to live up to her family's expectations. She had been driven to living on the streets, had become hooked on drugs, and eventually had to go into prostitution to survive.

The girl described how unnatural her spiral downward was. No one takes the step from a fairly normal life to being a drug addict and a prostitute in a day. Any sane person would consider that to be ridiculous, but it doesn't happen that way. Instead, you take one step in this direction and another step over here, and gradually you slip farther and farther down a chute. Before you realize it, you find yourself in a situation that you never dreamed would happen.

Geraldo Did Some "Real Life" Research

As I sat fascinated, listening to the girl talk about her experiences, Geraldo broke in with a little extra surprise for his viewers. He told his television audience that as he walked to the studio, off Times Square in New York, that day, he asked two young girls who were on the streets to turn tricks to go with him to talk about who they were and why they did what they did.

The two girls were ushered onto the stage before the cameras. They stood there, looking thin and emaciated. Geraldo pushed up their sleeves and showed their veins, wasted and bruised from drug injections. Then he asked one of the girls, "Why do you do this?"

"What else can I do?" she wanted to know. "Who is going to help me?"

The camera zoomed in on her face. I looked deep into her pain-filled eyes, and I found myself on the floor of my hotel room, weeping for those girls and for a generation of people like them, who live on the streets with no hope.

Those two children were not glamorous call girls who had rolled up to the studio in their Mercedes, wearing their fur coats. Their prostitution was a matter of life and death. They didn't want to live like that, but they saw no other choice.

I found myself praying for those girls, one of whom had twins just two years old. She had no idea who the father was. This wasted, sick child was the mother of two tiny lives, and she had to make enough to support them as well as herself. Half the money she made as a prostitute went to feed her children, and the other half went for drugs.

As I knelt there on the floor, I felt as if God had let me see a little shadow of the pain that He feels every day as He looks across the streets of America and sees the desperation. I stayed on the floor for a long time, praying for those two young girls and everyone they represented.

I could not forget those girls. Two nights later, I was doing a concert in Clearwater, Florida, and in the middle of the second half of my program I decided to talk about what I had seen on the "Geraldo" show. I had no idea that the emotion that had driven me to my knees two days before would come rushing back. But it did, and I couldn't go on. I don't usually cry in my concerts, but I couldn't help myself.

I paused, thinking, *Okay, I'll just take a second here and pull myself together*. But then I realized that I wasn't in control anymore, and there was nothing I could do.

I told the crowd, "I'm sorry. I know you've paid to come to a concert, but it just blows me away when I think about how God must feel about these young girls."

And Then God Took Over

I got down on my knees, right on the platform, with all those people staring at me, and I began to pray. After a minute or two I looked up, because I could hear the clearing of throats and quiet blowing of noses. The whole front of the church was filled with people who had come forward to kneel or fall flat on their faces. I could hear people asking God to forgive them for their apathy and unconcern. Some were crying out to be saved, and I almost felt like saying, "Excuse me, I haven't gotten to the salvation part yet."

After a while I stood up and read from Psalm 139:

> Lord, you have examined me.
>> You know all about me.
> You know when I sit down and when I get
>> up.
>> You know where I go and where I lie
>> down.
>> You know well everything I do.
> Lord, even before I say a word,
>> you already know what I am going to
>> say.
> You are all around me—in front and in
>> back.
>> You have put your hand on me.
> Your knowledge is amazing to me.
>> It is more than I can understand.
>
> Where can I go to get away from your
>> Spirit?
> Where can I run from you?

159

> If I go up to the skies, you are there.
>> If I lie down where the dead are, you are
>> there.
> If I rise with the sun in the east,
>> and settle in the west beyond the sea,
> even there you would guide me.
>> With your right hand you would hold
>> me. (Psalm 139:1–10)

I sang only one more concert number, "God Loves You." Then I ended the evening with a prayer. But that didn't end the evening at all. God was there, speaking to people.

A Vietnam veteran was bitter and angry because he'd come home and found people who didn't seem to care. But he found Jesus there that night and was able to forgive.

A little eight-year-old girl said to me, "I love the Lord. My mom's not a Christian; will you pray with me?" So I joined hands with her and her little friend, and the three of us prayed for her mother.

Young couples having trouble with their marriages came forward to talk. One person after another reached out to communicate with God—and to be honest and real, totally open to Him.

Fear Can Stifle Compassion

The best part of that evening in Clearwater was that I genuinely knew it was the Lord at work, and not me. I am not always holy or compassionate. Sometimes I hear Jesus' call to love the unlovely, but I let those ever-present traps of fear and selfishness keep me from answering that call.

I can recall a Saturday afternoon when I was in a small town where I was to give a concert in an old theater. The promoter told me not to wander too far away, as we weren't in a very safe area, but I was desperate for a cup of tea. After my sound check, I looked outside the theater and realized that only a few doors down was a place where I could get some hot tea to go.

Quickly I walked to the little restaurant, ordered my tea, and was hurrying back to the theater when I saw a man coming toward me. He must have been in his early twenties, and I could tell from the way he was dressed that he lived on the streets. His hair was very matted and dirty. His clothes were dirty and torn. He didn't have any shoes on his feet, and he had a strange look in his eyes.

As the wild-looking man got closer, my heart began to thump. Then he stopped me and said, "Can you give me something to drink?" I quickly thrust my hot tea into his hands and raced back to the safety and security of my dressing room. Then I forgot all about him.

That evening, the concert went well. Afterward, as I was counseling some people who had come forward to receive the Lord, I saw that same man in the crowd being counseled by some teenagers! After he wandered out, I went up to the two young people who had been talking with him, and I asked, "Do you know that man?"

They told me that as they were coming to the theater they had seen him on the streets and realized that he needed God's love. They stopped and asked him if he would like to come to the concert with them, and he said, "Sure, why not?" So they bought him a ticket and took him inside. Because his shirt was so torn and dirty, they also bought him a "Sheila Walsh" sweatshirt, which was on sale along with my tapes and CDs.

He put on the sweatshirt and then sat through the concert, listening intently. At the end he came forward to give his life to Jesus.

The two young people finished their story by explaining that, after leading him to the Lord, they had made arrangements to pick him up the next morning at a men's hostel, where he was staying, and take him to church.

I listened quietly as the two youngsters—a boy and a girl—shared their excitement with me. Then they disappeared into the night, rejoicing, and I was left in the strange quietness that lingers in a theater after everyone has gone home.

I sat and thought about our opposite reactions to the wild-eyed young man. I had seen him as a threat, someone who was different from me, someone who was unpredictable, possibly dangerous. The young people looked into his eyes and saw someone who needed Jesus, and they reached out to love him.

Then it struck me: That young man was like the fellow in the Bible who had been waylaid by robbers and left bleeding by the side of the road. Life had done exactly the same to him, but I, like the priest and the Levite, had walked past to go into the comfort of the theater and present the good news of the gospel to those who already knew. The young people, however, had cared enough to be good Samaritans, to bind him up and bring him in and share the love of Christ with him.

I think it's important to remember that Jesus told the story of the good Samaritan in answer to the lawyer's question, "Who is my neighbor?" This simple story, which almost every Christian knows by heart, surely shows that we may find ourselves in situations where we need compassion, but we might not always get it. Those whom we think will offer it do not, and when compassion does appear, it comes from unlikely neighbors, indeed. I met one of those unlikely neighbors myself while on that concert trip to Florida.

Compassion Is a Two-way Street

When our plane landed at the airport before the Friday night concert in Clearwater, I began to have despairing thoughts about the capriciousness of scheduling. Why had I ever agreed to do a concert after spending three days doing eleven "Heart to Heart" shows and two "700 Club" broadcasts? I had gotten up at 3:30 A.M. every morning, and I was beat. Why couldn't I just go home and sleep until Monday of next year?

All day Friday I was so tired I couldn't seem to get my program for that evening organized. But I did the best I could and went over to the church for a sound check late that afternoon.

As I finished, someone from a local radio station poked his head around the corner of my dressing room and said, "I'm here for the interview that we called about."

I looked at him aghast. The last thing I felt like doing at that moment was a radio interview. But I remembered having agreed to it, so I said, "Oh, sure, come on in."

He came in, sat down, took one look at me, and said, "You know, I can see you really don't need to be doing this."

"What do you mean?" I asked as I tried to pull my professional self together.

"Well, to be honest, you really look beat. Let's not bother doing this."

"Do you really not mind?" I asked, not believing my ears.

"No, you look like you need to rest and have a cup of coffee."

He went out. He came back with a cup of coffee he had found somewhere and sat down in the dressing room with Norman and me. After a minute or so, I said, "Can I ask you a favor? Would you pray for me?"

"Yes, I'd be glad to pray for you," he said.

I couldn't even tell you the man's name. He was from a local Christian station, in his middle to late thirties, and obviously a very kind and compassionate person. His prayer for me really touched my heart. He wasn't just somebody trying to get his job done, somebody who wanted his pound of flesh. He cared more about how I felt than getting his interview, which is not typical of members of the media. Usually it's a case of "We don't care how tired you are; we need this for the 6:00 news."

I believe God had given this young man the gift of compassion. Whether we are gifted or not, we can all learn to be more compassionate, not only toward the poor, the downtrodden, and the unlovely, but also toward our own families, friends, and acquaintances. Again, the book of Job contains rich truth for our taking.

Job Didn't Receive Much Compassion

As I read the book of Job I don't see his friends showing him a lot of compassion. Shock and dismay, yes. Willingness to spend time with him, yes. But not compassion. Instead, their words were laced with accusation, argument, and judgment. True, they sat with him, for seven days and seven nights. But then they wanted Job to confess the great sins that caused his incredible calamities. When he did not, they turned on him with scorn, indignation, and sarcasm.

In frustration, Job cried out:

> I have heard many things like
>   these.
>   You are all painful comforters!
> Will your long, useless speeches never end?
>   What makes you keep on arguing?
> I also could speak as you do
>   if you were in my place.
> I could shake my head at you.
> But, instead, my words would encourage
>   you.
>   I would speak words of comfort to bring
>   you relief. (Job 16:1–5)

Job must have felt terribly let down by his friends, who showed him no compassion to speak of. They only wanted to argue and prove him wrong, when they knew nothing of the agony that he was suffering.

When we look at Job's "miserable comforters" (and some of our own responses), we can see clearly what compassion is not. But what is it, then? My "synonym finder" tells me that compassion is showing pity, mercy, sympathy, kindliness, and concern. But I like the way Job put it: "I would speak words of comfort to bring you relief." Job was saying that if he were our friend, he would cry with us, hug us, or hold us. He would show us God's love and help us through our grieving process.

Job's response to his unhelpful friends reminds me that the days of the "Lone Ranger" are over. Each one of us needs to have friends who will care for us, even when we don't deserve to be cared for. Real friendship means that even when someone falls and makes mistakes, we are still there for them. Our relationships are not up for negotiation. One of the secrets to holding onto heaven when hell is on your back is to have friends who know God and love Him. Then they can reach out to know and love you as well.

The ultimate meaning of compassion is love and grace. When we grasp what God's love and grace have done for us, we cannot help showing compassion to others.

Harry Wondered Why He Had Lost Everything

One of my recent "Heart to Heart" guests was Harry Wingler, whose story would touch anyone. It wasn't so much his story that impressed me, as the compassionate people who were guest players on his stage.

Harry had been a very successful businessman, with his own bakery, employing twenty-six men. He was married and had two beautiful kids, but he began drinking and experimenting with drugs, and so did his wife.

Eventually, his wife left him, and the last he heard of her, she had died in the gutter as a prostitute. Local authorities moved in and took his two children away to put them in foster care.

From that moment, Harry rapidly spiraled downward. He got into financial trouble due to alcohol and drug abuse and found himself living rough on the streets. Once a well-dressed man, he now lacked a clean set of clothes to put on.

Eventually, Harry wound up living under a bridge, scraping through garbage cans, looking for some way to feed himself. He got hold of a gun, and he and a friend would rob homes. But the few dollars they made stealing were never enough. Harry's appetite for alcohol and drugs kept him penniless, homeless, and miserable.

One night he was sitting on a park bench, destitute, cold, and very wet. A young Hispanic kid from a local church came up and put a tract into his hand, saying, "Tonight we have a church service. Why don't you come? God could change your life."

The kid made Harry angry. He thought, *If there really is a God, why is my life like this? Why is everything such a mess? Why have I lost everything that ever meant anything to me?*

Nonetheless, something drew him to that church. As he stood outside, he could hear the music. It sounded as if they were all having a good time. It was cold outside, and it looked warm in there, and so he wandered in.

He sat at the back with his gun in his pocket, watching the people singing and praising God in this small Hispanic church. The pastor looked out at him from the pulpit and told him, "God can change your life, if you will let Him."

A woman who was sitting beside him fell to her knees and began to weep, crying out, "God, save my brother! Save my brother!"

"I thought she was crazy," Harry told me. I said to myself, *I'm not her brother. I'm not Hispanic. I'm not even a close relative!*

But Harry couldn't leave. Something about the love in that place held him fast. And before he realized it, he found himself at the front of the sanctuary, down on his knees, crying. The pastor prayed for him, and Harry, the once proud businessman who had fallen to living rough on the streets, gave his life to Jesus Christ and was filled with the Holy Spirit.

As he told me his story, so many years after it had happened, the tears rolled down his face, as they did mine. His eyes filled with such a radiance and a joy as he remembered the night when he stepped from darkness into light, as he remembered the radical change that God's love brought into his heart.

For me, however, this is where Harry's story really begins. The same night that he found salvation, Harry thanked his Hispanic friends and turned to leave. And they said to him, "Where are you going, Harry? You don't have a home. You're our family, now. You come and live with us."

One of the church families took him in, and he lived with them for weeks. Then the young people in the church, realizing that he didn't have anything nice to wear, chipped in their own money to buy Harry a brand-new suit of clothes.

After a few more weeks, they said, "Harry, you really need to get grounded in the Word of God." So they sent him off to Teen Challenge, where for seven months he studied the Word of God.

On that Thursday morning, with the television cameras rolling, I found myself sitting beside a man whose roots went deep into the Word of God. He reminded me of the man in Psalm 1 who was no longer walking in the counsel of the ungodly, but whose roots went down deep into the river of life. As Harry left that day, I hugged him and told him what a blessing he'd been to me as well as to the viewers. Driving home later, my mind filled with questions.

What would have happened had Harry come into one of our nice, white, middle-class churches? Would we have loved him the way that small Hispanic community loved him? Would we have taken him home?

Would I have taken him home to live with Norman and me? Would I have bought him a new suit of clothes? Or would I have gone home rejoicing that night that some homeless person had come to Jesus? Would I have sent him "home," back under that bridge, to have his quiet time?

Finally, I wondered, *If the people in that church hadn't loved Harry and gone on loving, would he have been here today with me?*

Some people might tell me, "Wait a minute, Sheila. It isn't us, it's Jesus. He is the One who draws and Who keeps and Who saves."

I know that, but I can't forget Harry's words: "You know, Sheila, so often we're prepared to take our hands off and say, 'Well, Jesus is the answer.'" Then he looked deep into my eyes and said something I'll never forget: "But you know, Sheila, *we're* the answer. You and me. Jesus has left us a job to do."

Harry Wingler reminded me that there is joy in doing God's will. A lovely old prayer by Ignatius of Loyola puts it this way:

> Teach us, Good Lord, to serve Thee as Thou deservest:
> To give and not to count the cost
> To fight and not to heed the wounds
> To toil and not to seek for rest
> To labor and not to ask for any reward
> Save the joy of knowing
> That we do Thy will!

St. Ignatius gave good advice. Unfortunately, we have become very self-indulgent and satisfied with our Westernized Christianity. We are in grave danger of staying within the comfortable confines of our own lives, failing to have compassion for others, and simply sitting at home to struggle with our own failures and temptations.

I appreciate the opportunities I've had to make missions trips to the Philippines, Poland, Russia, Bangkok, and Hong Kong. In countries like these, I've met people in desperate poverty but who are still rich in Christ.

I am also grateful for needs I have been able to see in the inner city among the elderly, the homeless, and unmarried pregnant girls. We can easily find places to share a cup of cold water right in our own community, sometimes right in our own block.

I am deeply thankful to God for bringing people like Harry Wingler across my path. He is just one of many relatively unknown people who have taught me a vital secret to holding onto heaven with hell on your back. That secret is compassion. When you reach out to others in the name of Jesus, you have to take your eyes off yourself. It is then that you suddenly realize you don't have to hold on at all. Because you are so close to Jesus, He has you in the hollow of His hand.

N I N E

When All of Heaven Is Silent

*When God seems far away
and our prayers bounce off the ceiling,
we can give in to despair, or we can keep
holding onto heaven in simple trust.*

No subject in this book tears at my soul more than what I want to share with you now. Across the land and around the world, thousands of believers pray fervently for healing, or perhaps just for relief from terrible pain or other difficulties. Every week calls from people in heartbreaking situations flood our "700 Club" phone lines.

The fifteen-year-old girl, living rough on the streets of Chicago, who asked me, "Can God be interested in someone like me?"

The eight-year-old boy who wrote to me: "You say that God can do all sorts of things. Please ask God if He'll make my mommy love my daddy."

The young man who told me he had been a homosexual for the past twelve years. When he told the elders of his church that he had given his life to the Lord and wanted to make everything right, they told him, "There is no place for homosexuals in our church."

The young girl who called me, saying she was being sexually abused by her father and her uncle, and she couldn't turn to anyone for help because no one would believe her.

The list can go on and on. There are innumerable situations where you want to see God's hand move and make a difference, make everything all right. Yet, heaven often seems silent, mute, uncaring.

Why?

I don't know the answer. I don't believe that anyone fully does. But God has brought some very brave and godly people into my life who have helped me understand that there are no easy answers and to accept living with mystery because they understand and accept when there is no visible reason to do so.

First, I want you to meet Debbie, a dear friend of mine who is a victim of the most debilitating form of multiple sclerosis. The first time I talked with Debbie was when she called the "700 Club" in the late summer of 1989 and asked for me. She told me a little bit about herself, how she had been a regular on her college volleyball team—the picture of health—and then one day the pain from MS started.

She told me she watched the "700 Club" every day, sometimes three times a day at different hours. But she admitted we were a mixed blessing: "I'm twenty-five; I'm dying of MS; and I'm scared. I love God, and I know ultimately I'm going to be in heaven—that's not the question. But I'm really scared, and you of all people should be the ones to help me. Why do you seem to be afraid to talk about the fact of death?"

I didn't have an answer for Debbie that day. I told her I would pray for her and that we would talk again—soon.

Debbie's call haunted me. The more I thought about it the more I realized that we could easily come across as if we were saying, "How dare you not get well? We've prayed for you. It can't possibly be our fault because we pray very good prayers. If you haven't gotten well, there must be something in your life, some kind of sin, that keeps you from being healed."

We're All One Happy Band, Until . . .

As the dog days of August passed, I looked forward to the special Labor Day services for everyone involved with CBN and Regent University. There are no broadcasts, and we all get together to fast and pray. Nonetheless, I couldn't get Debbie's agony out of my mind. She was dying by millimeters each day, and our broadcasts seemed at times to be pouring acid in her wounds in the name of the Lord.

Toward the end of our Labor Day time together, Pat Robertson got up to give his annual message on what he believed God had ahead for the "700 Club." Before he spoke he said, "If you have something on your heart you feel God has given you, I want you to come up and share it now."

I stood up and began to talk about Debbie—how much she loved the "700 Club," yet also had such real doubts and fears. Then I said:

"As I was praying about Debbie just yesterday, a picture came to my mind—a very clear impression of how we as a church march along like a very triumphant, happy little band, and any time members of our band fall down, we pick them up, dust them off, and give them a quick prayer. If they recuperate, they continue marching along. If they don't, they fall behind, but we don't even know. We never look back to see if they have made it or not. If they come with us, fine, but if they don't, it's their problem.

"And what does the Lord think of all this? I could imagine His saying: 'This must never happen. I'm tired of coming along behind you to pick people out of the gutter when that's really your job. It's time that you carried them because that's what the Christian walk is all about. If I choose to heal them, I will. If not, I want them to go from your arms to Mine; don't drop them by the wayside.'"

All across the room there was an awful hush, and I could hear one or two people sobbing. "Thank you, Sheila," Pat said quietly. "That was a good word." And then he led a prayer for all the people who were hurting, for those who were bewildered, waiting for God to answer their prayers.

I know our Labor Day experience together made us all more sensitive to those who face long-term or terminal illness. Since then we have done several specific shows on death and dying, and I am sure we will do more.

When I Saw Debbie, I Was Shocked

But that's not the end of Debbie's story. Not long after we met on the phone, her mother wrote to me: "If you want to do anything for Debbie, now's the time because we only have a few more months at the most. Is there any way I could bring her in for a weekend to meet you in person and talk with you?"

I called, and we made arrangements to have Debbie come, accompanied by her mother. When I saw her in the studio audience of the "700 Club" that day, I could not conceal my shock. Debbie was thin, pale, with dark circles surrounding her eyes. She looked so fragile, as if a puff of wind would carry her away.

As we became acquainted, I could see that for Debbie everything was a tremendous effort, even breathing. She is fed through a tube that has to be replaced every three weeks, and she told me of the terrible discomfort involved every time the tube has to be put down her throat into her stomach. Her doctor is a very compassionate man, and each time he starts to insert the tube, he tells her, "You know I love you, Debbie."

Recently, while trying to change the tube quickly, with as little pain for her as possible, he got it jammed and it started choking her. He tried to yank it back out, but it would not move. While still conscious, she could hear him calling for a gurney to get her to the operating room.

They rushed her down the hall, still conscious and thinking, *I'm dying. I've only a couple of minutes. . . . I know I'm dying.* Once in the operating room, there was no time to give her an anesthetic. The doctor simply took a scalpel, opened her stomach, and pulled out the tube. Then to numb the pain, he gave her a massive dose of something similar to morphine.

Debbie survived that incident, but every three weeks she knows it could happen again.

I asked her, "In the midst of something like that, where is God? In the midst of the panic, where is He?"

Debbie shared honestly with me about her fears and her disappointment in having so few Christian friends or church members who were willing to talk with her about her plight.

"Surely the church should be the one group of people who could help me die," she told me. "But they're the people who don't want to talk about it because they feel it's a lack of faith. I think it's because they're afraid. Why should I be afraid of heaven? Heaven is supposed to be such a great place, why should I be afraid? I ask them, 'Why won't you walk that way with me?'"

At one point I said to her, "Do you ever wish you'd just die?"

She nodded her assent and explained, "Three times I've prayed, 'Please take me now.' But then out of the corner of my eye I would see my mother, hanging in there, willing me to make it, and I would make myself make it for her sake."

She Never Feels Abandoned

Debbie and her mother have come to see me twice, and we talk often on the phone as well. They have both become my good friends. Debbie, always thinking of others, asks me, "Will you be there for my mom when I'm gone? Will you be there for my mom?"

We've talked about the funeral, what should be done and how. Through it all, Debbie is very honest, very real, and full of incredible faith.

In the last few days, as I have worked on this chapter, Debbie and I talked on the phone, and she told me of how her condition continues to deteriorate. She has such trouble breathing that oxygen has been installed by her bed so she can take it when she feels she needs it. But she's had a couple of frightening incidents when she had the oxygen up as high as it would go, and she still didn't seem to be able to breathe.

"I couldn't even tell it was on," she said. "My pulse was weak, and my mom was standing there. I could see terror in her eyes. She wanted to call for an ambulance, but I didn't want to die in a hospital. I knew this was it. I knew I was going, and I wanted to die at home. But when I saw how scared my mother was, I realized I couldn't put her through this."

Debbie was taken to the hospital that night, and the doctors were able to stabilize her condition. But she lives from day to day, her bones so weak and fragile that she can dislocate her hip if she brushes against something. Her left arm is in a cast because she broke it by just bumping against a wall.

I asked her if she felt abandoned during the moments when she thought, "This is it!"

She said, "I know for sure that if I did die, it would be okay. I've never felt abandoned. In fact, the funny thing is that I feel closer to Jesus at these times, but I'm still scared. There are still so many scary elements. I look at the anguish in my mother's eyes, and I know how she wants to hold on to me one more day. But over and above all that, there is a peace, and I know that if this is the moment that I'm going to die, it will be okay."

Debbie Asks the Searching Questions

I treasure the letters Debbie has written to me because they state so beautifully the hopes, fears, and incredible faith of someone who is dying slowly and in great pain, but who trusts God anyway. In one of her letters, Debbie asked the questions that puzzle all of us:

Why me?

Does God hear my prayers?

Why are some people healed and others are not?

Is my faith strong enough?

Why did it seem *at first* that I was all alone?

Debbie answered these questions from the perspective of someone who has every reason to give in to despair—but doesn't.

She said: "Through all of my illness, I have had so many questions and thoughts going through my mind. I've tried very hard to find some answers, and, although I will never know all the answers, I have come to be more comfortable with some of the very many struggles that being terminally ill brings."

"Why Me?"

"I never really have said, 'Why me?'" she continued. "If this had to happen I'm glad it has happened to me and not to someone I love among my family and friends. I go through a lot of pain, but I know I should never complain because it could never compare to the pain of Jesus Christ on the cross."

"Does God Hear My Prayers?"

"I used to ask myself, 'If God knew I would lose anyway, why did He make me try so hard to win?' In struggling with this issue I've come to the conclusion that there are times when, regardless of the score, just to be alive is to be winning.

"I used to think that maybe my faith wasn't strong enough. As you know, when I got down on my knees to pray I got the dislocated hip. I guess that's what I get for being bound and determined. When I pray it comes right from the heart, and I do appreciate and thank God for *every* day.

"I'll take the good and the bad, I want to live. You would think that I'd get used to all this frustration, severe pain, drastic change of life, and the long lonely times I have to sit in bed thinking of what it's all about while I have tubes and bottles and needles stuck in my body. I don't think you ever get used to it, at least I don't, but I do know while all this is happening I keep my personal relationship with Jesus Christ—a very honest open relationship.

"I know that at the times when I have not been able to walk, talk, move, even breathe on my own, God has carried me."

"Why Are Some People Healed and Others Not?"

"My life has kind of been like walking through the snow— every step shows. I wonder how many people feel the way I do about not being healed. I know that I am not alone, and I want to be an example to people to let them know that it's worth holding on. Yes, it does get hard and, yes, it's an up and down situation. But overall, life is worth living.

"If I knew that I've helped even one person—then I would be happy and feel like I've done what I've set out to do. Sometimes I wonder if God isn't giving me this time to reach out to others in similar situations. I feel as if there is something I still have to accomplish before I die. I pray I can. I want others to know they must accept Jesus into their lives so they can have eternal life.

"As I always say, only those prepared to die are really prepared to live, and as one of my favorite songs says, 'It is well with my soul.'

"I'd like people to say they are *living* with their diseases, not dying from their diseases. We have to know that being terminally ill is not a punishment from God."

"Is My Faith Strong Enough?"

"Since I was told that I do have a disease and that I am going to die, I have had a new way of looking at life. I realize how fragile life really is. At first I took a quick look at the Lord and a long look at my problems. I've learned to change this around, and now *I take a quick look at my problems and a long look at the Lord.*"

"Why Did It Seem at First I Was All Alone?"

"My illness has taught me many lessons, some very painful. Being terminally ill brings many changes in our lives, life-styles, families, and friends. My family has never left me. They have always stuck by my side, always pulling for me, and for this I am ever so blessed. Most of my so-called friends have not stuck around and have decided to let me go through this whole, long, painful ordeal alone with my family. I guess most can't face the fact that I am going to die, but I wish they would realize that someday they are going to die, too, and that I'm still the same old me, maybe just a lot more fragile and thinner, but I still think the way I always have.

"I got sick at a time in my life when I was just beginning to live. I had a lot of expectations: to be married, to have kids of my own, to be able to pursue a career, to be able to take care of myself, to raise my own kids the same good way I have been raised, to be able to give back some of the joy I have received in my life.

"I think a lot of my expectations have been crushed. I will never be called "Mom" by my own children. My mom and dad and sisters take care of me, including dressing me, helping me with medicine, IVs, injections, tubes, oxygen, feeding machines. Again, for this help I am very blessed.

"I've also learned that you should never take things for granted. Life is too short and fragile. I used to be very afraid of going to sleep at night because I was afraid I wouldn't wake up. I can't tell you the many, many nights I've lain in bed, thinking so many thoughts and saying so many prayers. Lately, I've decided to start saying, 'If I should wake up before I die.' It helps."

Every night Debbie goes to sleep with the hell of MS on her back, but she holds onto heaven by trusting God. Relatively few of us face, or will ever face, the pain and suffering Debbie and her family have experienced. Most of us, however, can relate to how it feels when all of heaven seems to be silent, and we see no solution to a hopeless situation. Many biblical personalities knew that feeling, particularly our good friend Job.

Don't Let Suffering Embitter You

Surely Job understood the feeling of abandonment that comes when the silence of heaven is deafening. He told his friend Eliphaz he could feel the arrows of an all-powerful God poisoning his being.[1] Like Debbie, he wished for death, but death did not come.

So anxious was Job for an audience with God that Job was willing to take his life in his hands and go before his Maker to plead his case rather than continue to listen to his friends smear him with their lies.[2] At one point Job said, "Though he slay me, yet will I trust in him" (Job 13:15 KJV).

Always, Job's real intent was to trust God *no matter what happened*. But as his suffering went on, day after painful day, he was driven to complain:

> I cry out to you, God, but you do not
>   answer.
>   I stand up, but you just look at me.
> You turn on me without mercy.
>   You attack me with your powerful hand.
> You snatch me up and throw me into the
>   wind.
>   You toss me about in the storm.
> I know you will bring me down to death. (Job 30:20–23)

Frustrated by God's silence and the continued attacks of the men who had come to be his "comforters," Job showed that he was very human, just like the rest of us. He couldn't understand why his prayers seemed to bounce off the ceiling. It seemed to him that God was attacking him without mercy. He wanted to trust God, but it all seemed so unfair.

It was at this point that Elihu came on the scene, and in his lengthy speech he gave Job a warning we all need to hear: "Watch out! Don't let your anger at others lead you into

181

scoffing at God! Don't let your suffering embitter you at the only one who can deliver you" (Job 36:18 TLB).

That's the answer I heard Debbie giving me in her letter. *God is the only One Who can deliver us, and we must trust Him.*

No matter what happens, no matter how inexplicable life can be, we must trust God, rather than give in to despair. I thank the Lord daily that in my work I meet people who model this kind of trust in amazing ways. I believe in miracles and have seen and talked with people who have experienced miracles. But the truth is, and Jesus demonstrated it again and again, miracles are not the real point. Jesus didn't do miracles for everyone. He didn't heal everyone. He performed healing miracles in certain situations to glorify God and to build the faith of those He touched. But always He wanted people to understand it is faith that honors God, whether miracles occur or not.

When pain and despair clamp down with jaws of iron, we wonder whether such faith is possible. Yet, I've seen Christians trust God when everyone else, even the healers and evangelists, have given up.

Randy Had Been Everybody's Guinea Pig

I met Randy, a young man in his early twenties, while singing in a missions convention in Hawaii. One of his legs was badly twisted from an accident he had had as a child. The main speaker at one of the evening meetings was to be a well-known Christian leader who had a reputation for extraordinary healing miracles. I was to sing first, and then he would speak. All day before the meeting, I kept thinking of Randy, who worked with a missions organization in the Hawaiian Islands. He loved God with a radiant faith and never questioned Him.

Wouldn't it be wonderful, I thought, *if Randy were healed—if tonight he ran right out of that meeting with his leg made whole?*

That night I finished singing and left the platform and sat down with high anticipation. During his message, the guest speaker said, "I want everyone in this place tonight who is not well to know it is God's will to heal every single person."

I could hardly contain myself. I was sure I was going to see an incredible miracle that would strengthen my faith as nothing else had ever done. The speaker assured us that he wasn't special and that he had no healing power. In fact, God could use any of us if we were willing, and then he offered an invitation to anyone who wanted to be able to pray for people so they could be healed to come forward.

Eagerly, I went to the front, and around two hundred other people joined me.

After the speaker prayed for us, he said, "If anybody is sick, I want you to come up and let one of these people pray for you."

A young girl came up to me and said she had a sore tooth, and I thought to myself, *Okay, God knows that I had better start with a sore tooth.* So I prayed for her, all the time trying to see over her head to where Randy was sitting. After I prayed, the girl said her tooth was better, and I thought, *That's great—that is really wonderful. . . .*

After much praying for those who had various ailments, there was a great deal of rejoicing and commotion as many said that they, indeed, were healed. Then the speaker moved on, the evening came to a close, and the speaker was whisked out a side door and was gone.

As the room emptied, I went about gathering up the tapes I had used for accompaniment while I sang. As I turned I saw Randy, sitting in a corner with his leg as twisted as ever.

I wondered what to do. Should I just slip out, or should I go over and talk to him? What would I say? But I couldn't worry about that. I knew I couldn't leave him because everybody had left him, and he was alone.

I sat down beside Randy and put my arm around him,

and we just sat there for a long time, not speaking. After probably ten minutes Randy finally said: "You know Sheila, you feel a lot worse than I do right now."

"What do you mean?" I said, not believing my ears.

"Well, I'm used to this. I've been everybody's guinea pig. I've had everybody who wants to be Kathryn Kuhlman pray for me. I've gone to healing meetings. I know God can heal me, and for a few moments tonight I thought maybe . . . *but my faith is not based on my healing. My faith is in Jesus.*"

Randy's words reminded me of what David Biebel wrote in his penetrating book *If God Is So Good, Why Do I Hurt So Bad?:* "Pain has two faces, human and divine. The human face is haggard, drawn, contorted and streaked with tears. The divine is calm, assuring, kind and loving, but likewise, streaked with tears."[3]

When I left Randy that night I had very mixed feelings. There was this tremendous sense of injustice and yet there was also the realization that Randy had been the strongest one in the room. And he had drawn his strength from only one thing: His faith was in Jesus, not in miracles, and he trusted God when He seemed far away.

Why Are We Afraid to Be Honest with God?

I've shared the stories of Debbie and Randy to make one point: For all of us, there will be times when God seems far away and prayers bounce off the ceiling. It is at these moments—whether we face terminal illness or are being terminated at work—that we must choose. We can give in to despair, or we can keep holding onto heaven in simple trust.

As I said in chapter 1, however, I believe that we can trust and still ask questions. To question God is not a lack of faith, although some Christians label it as that. When someone close to them is hurting, they seem to feel the need to contain their pain. They want to gift wrap it because the force of that pain might make them question their own faith.

Questioning God sounds blasphemous to some people. They might say, "How dare you? Who do you think you are, that you can come before God and question Him?" But I don't think being honest with God is blasphemous at all. I believe God wants us to be honest because He wants a real relationship with us, not something plastic or half-hearted.

Because my husband and I have been through so much together, today we have a wonderful relationship. It's wonderful because it is so real. Sometimes, for example, we can be in a crowded place where there are lots of other people. Somebody may say something, and I can look at Norman and he at me, and we both know what the other is thinking.

When I see that Norman has something on his mind, all I have to do is look into his eyes and ask, "Is something wrong?" In years past, when we struggled with communication, he would tell me, "Oh, no, everything's fine," and I would feel cheated. But now I know Norman always tries to be honest with me, and he knows that I try to be honest with him.

I sometimes ask myself how it must feel to be God and love people with a passion that would cause You to give Your only Son to hang on a cross and be ripped in two. How must it feel to know that that kind of love is the very essence of Your being; yet, day after day, You can see that Your children are hurting, but they only come before You to simply say, "Well, thank You, Jesus, for another day." They never open up. They are never honest. How that must grieve God's heart!

David Biebel made an apt observation when he said: "Why are hurting people sometimes asked, expected or required to pretend about the way they really feel when telling the truth is closer to godliness than pretending will ever be?"[4]

185

I believe God much prefers to have His children come before Him and say, "God, this makes no sense to me. I hurt so badly. I just don't understand. I don't think I'll ever understand, but, God, I love You and I trust You and I rest in the fact that You know how I feel. You've been there. You've had Your heart ripped out. I can't understand what is happening to me, but help me to glorify You through it all."

I want to end this chapter with the story of Marolyn Ford, a woman who kept on trusting God even though her prayers seemed to bounce off the ceiling year after year. Marolyn is one of those people who patiently wait for God's answer to come. Her story has the same happy ending as Job's, who was twice as well off after he withstood Satan's attacks and chose to accept whatever God gave him.

She Was Blind and Now She Sees

At the age of eighteen, Marolyn Ford found her sight beginning to fail. Soon she had lost all of her central vision and could no longer read or write, recognize people, or drive a car. All that remained was a little peripheral vision that made her aware of light and good-sized objects nearby.

She was examined at the Mayo Clinic, and the diagnosis was macular degeneration, which had ruined the retina in both eyes. Doctors were sorry, but nothing could be done. She would be blind for life.

A committed Christian since the age of nine, Marolyn had started praying for a godly husband at the age of twelve. She knew God wanted to use her in ministry of some kind, and she was sure she was supposed to marry a minister.

Marolyn went on to college, but not to a school for the blind. She gained a degree, completing her studies by listening to tape recordings of lectures, taking oral exams, and spending untold extra hours to pass all of her courses with excellent grades.

While in college she met the man who would become her husband. They married and had a daughter. By then, even the tiny bit of peripheral vision she had left had vanished, and she was totally in the dark.

Throughout her entire ordeal, Marolyn kept her inner eyes on Jesus, realizing that she would have to go on with her life. She says, "If you're going through the valley, through the tribulation, accept it as from the Lord. I didn't have to like my blindness, but I needed to learn to accept it. I knew the Lord had a reason for it, and my prayer was, 'Dear God, if I have to be blind, that it would not be in vain.'"

While Marolyn was willing to accept whatever happened, she often asked God to give back her eyesight. Each time she and her husband prayed, they were reminded of the apostle Paul. He had an affliction—some say it was of the eyes—and he prayed that the Lord would take that affliction from him. But each time he prayed it seemed that the Lord would say, "My grace is sufficient for you." And each time Marolyn and her husband prayed, it seemed as if the Lord were saying, "No Marolyn, I have a reason for you to be blind."

"I Can See! I Can See!"

Marolyn and her husband knew the Lord could heal. They continued to trust, believe, and hang on. One night after coming home from church, where Marolyn was the choir director, they got down on their knees to pray once again. Her husband cried out to God, asking Him for healing of Marolyn's eyes. Suddenly, inexplicably, miraculously, Marolyn could see perfectly. She shouted, "I can see! I can see!"

Her husband said incredulously, "What do you mean, you can see? You mean you can make out some dim objects or something?"

"No, I can see your face. I can see you. I can see everything!" For the first time she could look into the face of the man she had married. For the first time she could see her darling little girl.

It was a total and wonderful miracle. Three days later, Marolyn went to see her eye specialist. She walked into the office as any sighted person would do and easily read his eye chart. Then he spent a great deal of time peering into her eyes with all of his various instruments.

Finally, he stepped back and said, "Marolyn, you walked in here and read the letters on my eye chart, and it's obvious you can see, but medically speaking your eyes are still blind. When I look into your eyes, all I see is black scar tissue where it should be smooth and pink. There is no medical explanation for why you can see with those two eyes."

At first, Marolyn was disappointed because she had thought that God had "healed her completely." But then she realized that the return of her sight was an even greater miracle. She has shared her story with thousands of people throughout the world, strengthening the faith of many Christians and bringing many other people into the kingdom. It has been almost ten years since the miracle, and she still thanks God every day that her blind eyes now see.

Marolyn Ford's testimony to me on "Heart to Heart" gave a real lift to my own faith. I believe with all my heart that God can do miracles, but I have never seen a miracle like Marolyn's occur right before my eyes. I pray for more faith to believe what God can do, but I also thank the Lord that so many other Christians have been models of faith and commitment, even though they have not been healed.

Whenever heaven seems to be silent, we face a critical choice. We can give in to doubt, frustration, anger, depression, and, finally, despair because the hell on our backs is just too much to bear. Or we can hold onto heaven, just as Jesus did when He faced Gethsemane, the mockery of a trial, floggings, crucifixion, and, worst of all, the moment when God turned His face from His Son.

Rebecca Manley Pippert was my guest on "Heart to Heart" recently, and she shared many helpful insights from her new book *Hope Has Its Reasons*. I strongly recommend that you obtain a copy, because it contains excellent counsel on what to do when all of heaven seems to be silent. Becky's words say it so well for Debbie, Randy, Marolyn—and all of us:

"Jesus' resurrection scars also prepare us for the fact that there may be pain in our lives, too. There may come a time when little makes sense and when evil and chaos seem to be winning the day. There may be times when we feel hopelessness and confusion, when we do not see even a flicker of light and the lesson of Jesus' scars is to hold on, to be patient and to trust God, even when we cannot see any reason to do so."[5]

T E N

There Is a Better Song to Sing!

When our dreams seem to go sour
or remain unfulfilled,
turmoil and hopelessness can dominate our lives,
or we can hold onto heaven with open hands,
ready to let God put in what He wishes
and take out what He wills.

According to the apostle Paul, there are three things that will continue forever: faith, hope, and love. Paul makes it clear that the greatest of these is love, and we all agree. But what of the other two?

We know faith is crucial. Without faith it is impossible to please God or to hang onto heaven when hell is on our backs. Doubt can creep in so easily, and the only answer is to remember that Jesus is worth it all.

But what about hope? In our haste to be sure we have faith and love, do we sometimes fail to give hope its proper due? Without hope, life is a sorry game, played without enthusiasm or joy.

As our society marches into the 1990s, people wonder what our *real* chances are. Is there any *hope?*

191

Those are legitimate questions, and I believe that only Christians have the legitimate answers. I was reminded of this not long ago in, of all places, a movie theater.

There Is a Place to Take Broken Dreams

I've always loved going to the movies, and I'm the kind of person who wants to see *all* of the film. If I miss the first minute, I won't go in. I'm worse than Woody Allen. I'll wait two hours until it starts again. I like to be already seated when the lights go down so I can get into the mood of the whole thing.

And I don't like to leave until all the credits have rolled. I want to know who the cameramen were, the key grip, and all the rest of the "little guys" behind the scenes who gave their all for that film.

That's why I love to go to the little arty theaters where everyone seems to feel compelled to watch all the credit lines roll at the end of the film, whether they like them or not. Most of the time in a regular cinema people just get up, wade through all the spilled popcorn, and leave the minute the film is over.

Recently, Norman and I went to see *Field of Dreams*. It's a fantasy story about a man who builds a baseball field in the middle of an Iowa cornfield, and somehow star ball players appear from the past to play on his field and give him new hope for his own life and broken dreams. The film's "theology" left a lot to be desired, but the story still had real impact on me.

As usual, when the film ended, I just sat there with Norman, trying to watch the credits while everybody kept walking past us on the way out. But as the house lights came up just a little, I couldn't help noticing the faces of the people going by. The women were smiling and chattering because they had enjoyed a good film and Kevin Costner's good looks.

But as I looked into the eyes of some of the men, I saw something else. In some of the older men, in particular, there was a look of regret. For two hours they had indulged themselves in an unfamiliar luxury. They had looked back and thought about their lives, and now they were thinking, *Maybe things could have been different.*

When these men were young, they were idealistic, but now they knew that life was a matter of compromise, because that's the way life goes. You have to give and take in everything. After seeing *Field of Dreams* and thinking about how some of their own dreams had crumbled, they had looks of doubt, of wondering for just a moment, *Was I right or was I wrong in how I lived my life?*

I saw this look in the eyes of many of the men who streamed past us on the way out of the theater, and it made me want to stand up and call them all back in. I wanted to say that you can go back. There is a place to take your disillusionment, a place to take all your regrets, all the things you wish could have been done some other way.

I wanted to say to them, "What can you do with your broken dreams? There is a place—at the foot of the cross—where there is room for new beginnings!"

How Rita Found Her Song

The longing look in the eyes of the men who came out of *Field of Dreams* that evening reminded me of another film I had seen years ago. It was called *Educating Rita,* the story of a young Liverpool housewife who began to realize she could make more of her life. She enrolled in a university and began to study. A whole new world was thrown open before her to explore.

Soon, however, she began to feel defeated, not accepted by her family or by the academic community at the university. One night she was invited to a dinner party at her professor's home, but upon arriving at the door and glancing in the windows at all the sophisticated, formally dressed guests, she decided she couldn't go in. She went instead to the pub to join her husband, her parents, and the rest of her family, who were drinking beer and singing old familiar songs in typical British fashion.

Rita tried to join in with the singing, but it was all so hollow and so predictable: the men were all getting drunk, with their obedient wives at their sides, trying to look as if they were having a good time.

As the songs continued and the beer flowed, Rita looked over and saw her mother. She had stopped singing and was sitting there with tears trickling down her cheeks. Rita's mom was an average British housewife who lived by the code, "Just grit your teeth and keep going." But there she was, crying quietly while her intoxicated husband sang at the top of his lungs.

"Why are you crying, Mother?" Rita asked.

Without hesitation her mother said, "There must be a better song to sing."

Her mother's words gave Rita new hope and resolve to keep going to school. She had been about to give up, because her husband had taken all her books and thrown them in the fire. He didn't want his wife to be smarter than he was. She was supposed to stay home and get pregnant—that was her job.

Instead, Rita returned to the university and told her professor, "That's what I'm trying to do, isn't it? Sing a better song. Well, that's why I've come back, and that's why I'm staying. So let's start to work!"

Rita had decided her better song would come through

finding herself through education. She would not give up, because there was, and always will be, a better song to sing.

A Better Song Grows in Brooklyn

Recently Norman and I found ourselves in New York City, where we planned to spend a weekend kicking back and doing very little. There was no concert, no business appointments. We did plan to attend church at the Brooklyn Tabernacle, pastored by Jim Cymbala, a man who had impressed Norman in the past with his simple but profound commitment to Christ. I was scheduled to provide some special music for the service, which I was happy to do.

"Sheila, you're going to love Jim," Norman told me. "He is a real man of God."

We spent Saturday just strolling around, doing a little window shopping. We stopped in at Trump Tower, where the price of a cup of coffee makes you wonder if you won't have to remortgage your home. It was a great day—a day to just relax and have fun.

On Sunday someone from Jim's church came by to pick us up and take us across from Manhattan into Brooklyn. It was a beautiful sunny day, and the church was packed. It seemed as if every race, creed, and color represented on the planet had found their way to the Brooklyn Tabernacle that particular Sunday.

The well-known Scottish poet Robert Burns once wrote, "The best laid plans of mice and men, gang aft agley." That means that you can plan all you like, but it doesn't mean it's going to happen the way you've planned. How true his words are! As I always do before a concert or church service where I'm singing, I had planned to arrive in plenty of time to do a sound check in peace and quiet before the crowd came in.

What I didn't know was that at Brooklyn Tabernacle, the worshipers come in hours before anything begins. There were people everywhere. They were up on the platform where the choir was rehearsing. They were yelling up at me from the pews, asking who I was and what I was doing up there. They were coming up behind me and hugging me. I was determined that I was going to do this sound check if it killed me, and it looked as if it just might.

I guess I don't have a lot of patience some days. I just need things to go right, and when they don't I'm not thrilled. Norman played the first tape through the machine and said, "Sheila, sing along." It was awful. The music sounded as if it were coming through a dirty football sock.

"I can't sing to this," I wailed. "I can't even hear it. It's terrible!"

"Well, just sing anyway," Norman urged me. "We'll all try to do our best. Maybe we can improve it as it goes along."

Suddenly, it seemed as if every eye in the church was looking up at me as if to say, "Is this who is going to be singing to us? We can't bear it!"

I tried to sing through the microphone, but it sounded as if I were strangling a large cat, and I had had it. I knew I had to get out of there so, keeping my head down like a good evangelical, I headed out through the crowd of people toward the front door of the church. I made it outside, and I stood there thinking, *Lord, what am I going to do? It sounds so terrible. I don't know what to say to these people. I just wish I could run away and hide somewhere.*

God Speaks in Special Ways

Then I felt someone put a hand into my hand and squeeze tightly. I looked down, and there was a little black girl; I suppose she was probably twelve years old. As I looked into her eyes, she grinned one of those grins that stretch from ear to ear and across the top of your head, and she said, "Isn't it great to know that Jesus loves us?"

Isn't there something about the truth coming out of the mouths of babes? I smiled back at her and tried to say something like, "Yes, sweetheart, it certainly is." Then I turned around and headed back into the church, thinking, *Well, I guess it's time to get off your high horse again, Sheila Walsh, and join the infantry. You'll just have to march down there with all the rest of the little soldiers and take your seat at the front.*

And then I prayed, "Lord, maybe this is going to be the worst thing they've ever heard, but I give it to You, and I ask that somehow You will touch these people, because already they have reached out and touched me."

The service began, and Norman was right about Jim Cymbala. He's a simple, honest, dynamic man of God. His message that afternoon, which has remained with me so clearly, emphasized the way in which you and I bring pleasure to God's heart. It was so real and so tangible, especially his assurances that no prayer ever prayed on this planet by God's people has been lost.

"The angels hold our prayers in golden bowls up before the Father, because the fragrance of our prayers is so sweet to Him," Jim told us. "And then the angels say to Him, 'Listen, smell, see Your children praying.'"

I wonder whether you've ever prayed and felt as if your words went no higher than the ceiling. You wonder because no answer seems to appear in the mail by the next morning. Did God really hear?

That day I prayed my own feeble prayer there in the front of the Brooklyn Tabernacle, saying, "Oh, Lord, again I've been reminded of my clay feet and my fallibility. If there's anything You can do through me today, then I'm Yours, and I ask that You would wash me again and make me clean."

At that moment I knew everything would be okay. I knew and believed with all my heart that every prayer ascends to the very heart of God and brings Him pleasure.

These People Needed a Different Song

As I stood up to sing, I began with one or two of my favorites from my albums. But as I sang, I looked out across the congregation and realized that so many of these people were living in desperate situations. These people lived in the harsh reality of life in one of the poorer areas of New York City. They were used to all sorts of abuse and suffering: cold, poverty, lack of food, and even violence. Jim had told me before the service that many of the women sitting there would stay long after worship was over because they knew the minute they went home, their drunken husbands would beat them.

As I looked into their eyes, I realized that my songs just weren't reaching them. They were nice enough—in fact, they were good words—but they didn't relate to where these people were. I just stopped in the middle of my presentation and said to Norman, "Look, I think we should scrap the rest of the tapes."

Then I turned around and said to someone on the platform, "Do you have a hymnbook?" I was handed an old hymnbook, and I quickly found what I was looking for in the index. Then I faced the crowd and began to sing:

> When peace like a river attendeth my way!
> When sorrows like sea billows roll;
> Whatever my lot, You have taught me to say,
> "It is well, it is well with my soul."

As the beautiful words of that well-loved hymn fell on the ears of the audience, I could see that all across the church

198

hands began to raise in worship. Some people were on their knees, tears rolling down old, well-worn faces.

That hymn, written by a man who had lost his wife and children in a terrible accident, reminded us again that whatever we face, whatever we go through, whatever changes or does not change, there is still a great truth that all God's people can embrace. Even in the darkness and disillusionment, when dreams are shattered, we can sing, "It is well, it is well with my soul."

And I learned again that morning that in any situation Christians always have a better song to sing. Because we have faith in Christ's loving sacrifice, we always have hope.

Van Gogh Was More Than a Painter

One of my most favorite personages from the world of art is the painter Vincent Van Gogh, whose life was dramatized in Irving Stone's novel *Lust for Life*, which was made into a film starring Kirk Douglas. If you read the book or saw the film, you know that Van Gogh was far more than a painter who became a tormented man, unable to live in the real world.

Early in his life he was an evangelist, and his mission organization sent him to a region in Belgium where the coal mine workers lived in desperate poverty. Van Gogh was provided with a nice house, but when he saw the shacks the miners were living in, he found it impossible to live in his much finer quarters.

He probably told himself, *If I'm going to reach them, I'm going to live as one of them.* And so he moved into a horrible shack, wore virtually nothing but a sack, and began to hold meetings. Eventually, people began to come to his meetings, and for six months he had an incredible impact in that area. Unfortunately, the head of his mission board came down for

199

a visit. When he saw how Van Gogh was living—as one of the poor and downtrodden—the man became so disgusted with Van Gogh that he fired him.

Van Gogh had to leave the people he was trying to help, but they never forgot his sermons, which included statements like: "For those who believe in Jesus Christ, there is no sorrow that is not mixed with hope." And Van Gogh also said: "It's an old belief and a good one that we are strangers on earth, yet we are not alone for our father is with us."[1]

Finally, Our Eyes Must See Only Him

One reason why Psalm 139 is one of my favorite passages is that it describes so beautifully how the Lord is always with us—every moment of every day and night. Every time I read it, it strengthens my hope because having hope is realizing that your destiny is interwoven with God's sovereign power and will for your life. As Job went through incredible suffering, he continued to wonder where God was. If only God would make Himself plainly known, then Job would have something to count on, something to keep his hope alive.

Toward the end of the story, God finally appeared in all His sovereign power and glory. After hearing a thunderous barrage of unanswerable questions from the Lord, Job admitted that he had talked about things that he did not understand and that he had spoken of things too wonderful for him to know. Job's confession was Satan's final defeat. The argument between Satan and God that opened the book of Job was settled once and for all because Job now said, "My ears had heard of you before. / But *now my eyes have seen you*" (Job 42:5, italics added).

And then Job added, "So now I hate myself," meaning that he hated his sin, which is what all of us must ultimately hate, no matter what life brings. As Job put it, "I will change

200

my heart and life and sit in the dust and ashes" (Job. 42:6).

Job had never received an answer to his first question—"Why?" Nonetheless, it was enough. Even in his pain Job had found a better song to sing because now he had gained a new understanding that his only hope was in God.

Blown in Half, He Became Whole

When I think of people God has brought into my life through my travels or on "Heart to Heart" conversations on television, I am reminded a little bit of the "Hall of Fame of Faith" listed in chapter 11 of the book of Hebrews. There are people great and small, known and unknown, who have had their dreams crushed and even ground to powder, but they have found hope—and God's better song.

I remember Bob Wieland, who went to Vietnam standing 6 feet tall and weighing 270 pounds of rock-hard muscle. Bob came home 2 feet 10½ inches tall and weighing 87 pounds after a Viet Cong mine blew him in half.

As Bob talked with me, he described so vividly what life was like for a young American soldier in Vietnam. His graphic descriptions made me feel the hot, sticky, noisy jungle and the fear of not knowing what lay around the next clump of bamboo. Bob told of the day that he and others in his platoon were making their way through the jungle. He could feel an unnatural stillness like the tension that builds in you when you watch a horror movie and you just know that something is going to jump out and stick a knife between someone's shoulder blades.

Suddenly, Bob heard one of his friends, who was walking just in front of him, scream. Bob began to run toward him, and that's all he can remember. He stepped on a mine that was big enough to blow away a tank; it threw his upper body one way and his legs another.

After the battle was over, Bob lay there for five days with most of his blood draining out on Vietnamese soil. When medics finally found him, they were sure he was dead, but Bob fooled them. Perhaps he didn't have any legs, but he was still alive and "kicking."

He remembers coming to and thinking, *Well, Lord, they tried to finish me off here, but I'm still alive. So what do You want me to do? What purpose do You have for my life?*

A natural athlete who had planned a professional career in baseball, Bob now realized that dream was over. Nonetheless, he decided not to lose hope. Instead, he would try something else. He became a weight lifter and trained day in and day out. Eventually he began competing and made it his new dream to establish a world record.

The big day finally came. Bib gripped 370 pounds and with one supreme effort lifted it above his head to establish a new world mark.

Before the dust of glory had a chance to settle on Bob's head, he got the news. His title was being taken away. He was disqualified because someone had discovered a rule on the books that said you had to wear shoes while lifting a weight in competition.

As Bob told me this story, I stared in disbelief and blurted, "What did you do? If you didn't snap at Vietnam, surely you had to snap now. You went out there to serve your country; you did what you felt was the right thing; you gave everything you had; and you lost your legs. You came back a different man, you work and train and get to the place where you can break a world record, and they tell you that because you had 'carelessly' left your legs in Vietnam you were disqualified."

Bob smiled and said simply, "What could I do? I looked in the judge's face, shook his hand, and told him, 'I understand. That's all right.'"

Bob Wieland showed me that morning that he grasps something that no book, other than God's Word, can teach: *No earthly crown is ultimately worth anything.* Bob Wieland decided to hold onto heaven with open hands that allowed God to put in what He wanted. I imagine that on the day when they took away his medal, in a quiet, unseen place, another jewel of far greater and more infinite value was placed in Bob Wieland's crown.

An Ultra-Marathoner with No Legs!

But Bob wasn't finished. He had a dream to do something for the homeless in America, and he decided that while he didn't have his legs, he did have his hands. He would "walk" across America to raise money for the homeless. Wearing special gloves that were built like shoes, Bob took off, propelling his weight with *nothing but his arms and hands* on a coast-to-coast journey that took three and a half years.

He went through all sorts of weather, discovering support from unlikely people and encountering opposition from others who were embarrassed by his so-called disability. One little eight-year-old boy came up to him and gave him twenty pennies he had in his piggy bank. Homeless people saw him, took out what little change they had, and gave it to him because they understood that he wanted to make a difference.

Everywhere he went, Bob asked God to give him an opportunity to speak to people about the difference that Jesus had made in his life. One day he had traveled mile after mile and had not seen a car, so he asked the Lord, "Before I go to bed tonight, could You just give me two people? Perhaps a car could stop, and I could develop an opportunity to talk to two people about You."

It was almost dusk when a car pulled up beside him and

an older couple got out. They talked with Bob for a long time about many things, and eventually Bob said, "Can you see any reason why you shouldn't give your lives to Jesus right now?"

The older couple said they could not, and they joined Bob there on the side of the road, on their knees, and prayed to receive the Lord as their Savior.

But there is one more thing about this story. I'm sure that as Bob lay in bed that night he had a grin from ear to ear. And perhaps there was a tear on his cheek because that older couple whom he had led to the Lord on that dusty road were his own mother and father. Now they also had a better song to sing, because for the first time, they had fixed their hope on Someone Who transcends all of life's disappointments and broken dreams.

Our hope in Christ enables us to come to God with open hands into which He can place what He wants and out of which He can take what should not be there. Just recently I realized that that is what God has done for Norman and me.

A Birthday Card for Norman

It was about 7:00 in the evening and because I knew Norman was working late, I decided to catch up on a few errands that had been on my list for over a week but had gone undone. One of those items was getting Norman a card for his birthday, which was the next day.

I found myself in a card shop, looking through rack after rack of cards. Eventually I found the one that said what I wanted to say. There was a beautiful picture of a husband and wife on the beach; it looked like Laguna at sunset, my favorite time of day when you don't have the glare of bright sunshine, and darkness hasn't quite crept in yet. The sun just hangs there for a moment between the two, and time seems to stop. The words inside the card conveyed my feelings perfectly:

> Every woman dreams about the perfect husband. Someone warm and caring, thoughtful and affectionate, funny and sensitive, and she often ends up with less, except me! When I married you, I ended up with a whole lot more! Happy Birthday!

And then I added, "With all my love, Sheila."

I stood there in the middle of that busy store on a busy evening and couldn't believe how far Norman and I had come. I thought back to the year before and the year before that when I had tried to find cards for him that were as non-committal as possible. Back then, all I wanted was something that would get me over the hurdle of a day that was supposed to be so special, but wasn't because it was shared between two people in pain. We were like two animals who lived in a cage, pacing around each other to find a way to coexist peacefully but afraid that at any moment the other would lash out.

There are times in our lives when we feel that we take baby steps. We feel that we make such little progress as Christians until a moment catches us unaware and we look back and realize that Jesus has carried us a long way down the road. Gratitude and praise just welled up in my heart because I'd found that perfect something to let Norman know how much I loved him.

I wanted to tell him how precious he is to me; how much I treasure him; that there is no one else on this planet with whom I would rather be alone. I wanted him to know I couldn't imagine spending my life with anyone else but him. And I prayed with all my heart that God would give us many years to laugh, to cry, and to grow wrinkled together. I wanted so much to do things that would make him happy. I'd already gotten him his "big present," but I had wanted that little thing that would mean something special to the two of us, which no one else would quite understand. As I walked up the aisle to pay for the card, I realized that when you give yourself away, when you look for a way to make the other person happy, you suddenly see your face in the mirror and discover that you're smiling.

In a simple but profound way, buying that birthday card reminded me of why keeping covenants with God is so important. And I also thought of Jesus' words: "Whoever wants to save his life will lose it, but whoever loses his life for me will find it" (Matt. 16:25 NIV).

There Is Always a Way Through

When the world asks if there is any hope, we can say, "Absolutely!" As Philip Yancey put it, "No one is exempt from tragedy or disappointment—God Himself was not exempt. Jesus offered no immunity, no way *out* of the unfairness, but rather a way *through* it to the other side."[2]

Yancey's words remind me of an illustration Corrie ten Boom used on many occasions. As she spoke, she would hold up the wrong side of a tapestry for her audience to see.

"Isn't this beautiful?" she would ask.

As the people looked at the back of the tapestry, all they saw were threads crossed at odd intervals, knotted in places, looking clumsy and disjointed. It was, to be blunt, ugly.

The audience would stare back at Corrie, not knowing how to respond to her question. Corrie would be silent for a few moments, and then she would say, "Oh! Yes, of course. You can't see the tapestry from my perspective."

Then she would turn the piece of cloth around to show the front, and there would be a picture of a beautiful crown!

During those moments when Norman and I struggled

with our marriage, all we could see were the knots and tangles we had woven into our life together. But God could see the front of our tapestry. He could see me on the beach at Kauai, making my decision to stay with Norman. He could see us falling in love again. He could see that birthday card I would buy and the love and joy we now share.

At times, life makes no sense. It seems disjointed, distorted, and ugly. But if we surrender our little view of life for God's much grander portrait, we will always be able to hold onto heaven and our eternal hope in Jesus Christ.

ELEVEN

One Life Does Make a Difference!

When we face our choices, large or small,
we can settle for lukewarm, diluted faith,
or we can seek the real thing, because we know that one life—
one Christian word or deed offered with unbridled zeal—
does make a difference now and through all eternity.

Every year, a week or two before Christmas, we hold what we call the Operation Blessing Banquet at CBN. It was born out of Pat Robertson's commitment to live out Jesus' parable about the man who gave a great banquet and invited many prominent guests. All of them made excuses about why they couldn't come, so the man decided to send his servants back into the streets and alleys of the town to bring in the poor, the crippled, the blind, and the lame—those who would never be able to pay him back.

At Christmas it's our goal to reach people just like the ones in the parable, people who don't have very much. At our last Operation Blessing Banquet, around 3,500 people were there from old people's homes and the "slum" areas of Virginia Beach. There were also many of the homeless who lived under freeway overpasses or who just slept on the streets.

Our program is always simple. We have a delicious turkey dinner, I sing, Pat speaks, and then we give everyone a Bible and other little gifts. One woman came with her three children and told us they all lived in a car, and this would be their only Christmas dinner.

But I remember most of all a black woman of around sixty who served as one of the hostesses at our table. I believe God gave me the privilege of just listening to this woman and learning from her life and her spirit.

Her name was Betty. She told me that her mother had only been fourteen when she had conceived Betty. Somehow Betty's mother had never forgiven her for being born. When she got old enough, Betty would say, "Mom, it's not my fault, I didn't have anything to do with it. *You* got pregnant."

Betty's mother was never able to tell Betty she loved her. And yet Betty told me that she still flies out twice a month to Tempe, Arizona, to see her mom and make sure she's all right.

As Betty told me about her life and her many hardships, which included three heart attacks, I sat in wonder. She had such a peace about her—a peace that could come only from walking with Jesus for many years. As the evening came to a close, I told her, "You know, Betty, when I meet a woman like you, I can see you have been through the fire."

Betty looked at me for a long moment and then said, "Sheila, never, ever forget that if that's what it takes to be like Jesus, *then let it burn!*"

As I looked into Betty's face, creased with cares I had never known, I knew I was in the presence of someone who fully realized that one life does make a difference. She had the same look that I had seen only a few months before on a trip behind the Iron Curtain, into the lair of the great Russian bear itself.

Faith Is Alive and Well in Russia

The events that have occurred recently in the Soviet Union, as well as in eastern Europe, have been almost unbelievable as millions have begun to shake off the yoke of Communism that has been around their necks for many decades. On the streets of Lithuania and at the Berlin Wall, we have seen on our television screens people with a new song to sing. But many months before all this occurred, Norman and I had the privilege of seeing Christians in Russia who had been quietly singing their own song for many years and who intended to go right on, no matter what became of the Communist regime.

In August 1989, Norman received a telephone call from Jim Groen, the International Director of Youth for Christ, who explained that YFC was planning to hold the first ever public Christian gathering in Estonia, one of the countries that had been absorbed into the Soviet Union and was now part of the Communist bloc. They wanted me to be a part of it, and, though the dates presented major problems, I agreed to finish up my work on the "700 Club" on a Friday, fly straight to New York with Norman, then board a plane for London and go on to Moscow. From there we could take another plane to Estonia, where I would sing that weekend in the special Christian celebration. Then we would travel back on Monday, and I would be ready for my usual "700 Club" appearance on Tuesday morning.

We arrived in Moscow without incident and had some crazy experiences with cab drivers that evening, as well as one of the most unusual "dinners" we had ever eaten. It consisted of roast bear and prunes. The bear that had given its all for our dinner had undoubtedly died of old age, and to be kind we would just have to say it was chewy, very chewy. Still, it seemed to be part of our whole adventure, and I thought it was fun. No salad, no dressing, no french fries, just bear and prunes.

The next morning, however, we had to be up at 4:30 to be at the airport by 7:00 to take off on our Aeroflot flight to Estonia. Since my natural preference is never to begin life before lunch, the early hour was torture, and along with feeling tired, I was nauseated. That bear was growling, and because the hotel hadn't started serving breakfast when we left, I couldn't even get a cup of tea to settle my stomach.

When we got to the airport, Norman tried to find some breakfast, but all they were serving was cold, thick, hard salami and *very* dark bread. There was no way I could eat that, so we boarded our Aeroflot flight, and I soon learned why experienced travelers call it "Aeroflop."

You sit in seats facing fellow passengers, all of whom have been allowed to take as many of their belongings as they wish. None of this "two items of hand luggage or you'll have to have it checked" business with Aeroflot! Some people looked as if they had brought along the entire contents of their homes.

Norman and I found ourselves separated. Sitting beside me was a Russian soldier who had apparently drunk enough Vodka to pickle the livers of his entire battalion. Opposite me sat a woman with a huge hairy dog that drooled over my feet during the entire trip. I don't remember ever finding my seat belt. I'm not sure if the drunken soldier was sitting on it or whether the dog had eaten it before I sat down.

We finally landed in Estonia, and a local pastor named Rein, who was also a Youth for Christ representative for the area, met us. He was just beaming from ear to ear as he hugged us and bundled us into his car to take us to the hotel. We found when we got there that there had been a mixup and our room wasn't ready, so we headed on over to do our sound check at the Lenin Cultural Auditorium. The sound system there was excellent, as was the lighting. It was a beautiful theater, very modern in every respect.

Later, Rein led members of his church in a prayer meeting before the concert began. Even though he was praying in another language, I have never heard anyone pray the way this Estonian pastor prayed as we all gathered around. Many people ended up on their knees in tears. He had such a passion for God that I almost felt as if I were intruding during a very private conversation. Then he prayed in English, intensely, passionately, very much in love with the Lord.

Afternoon and evening performances had been planned, and the theater soon began to fill. Before the weekend would be over, we would minister to over twenty thousand people. It all began by bringing in the Estonian Children's Choir to sing the national anthem, which up until recently had been against the law. Even then, Communism was beginning to weaken.

As I stood in the wings watching, I could see people across the audience weeping with the sheer joy of being identified publicly as Christians.

That afternoon I did my part of the program, and everyone was very warm and polite. Later that evening I was given an hour, during which I sang, shared favorite verses of Scripture, and told how I met the Lord and what He meant to me. I spoke through an interpretor, a man named Tor, who spoke so fast it seemed that when I said my words he said them right behind me in Estonian. He even got in the emotions and inflections, and it seemed as if we were just one voice.

When I finished, the entire audience stood and applauded as if they would never stop. I didn't know what to do. I was embarrassed, but also overwhelmed by their warmth and love, which washed over me like waves. Over that weekend, two thousand people streamed forward to find Christ for the first time.

Afterward, two other local pastors came backstage to thank me. As we talked, I asked them, "Do you pray that someday your children will grow up and be able to come to the West, to freedom, to a better life?"

They looked at me and just smiled. They weren't angry with me, but they were a bit surprised, perhaps even shocked, that I would ask such a question.

"No," one of them explained. "We pray that our children will grow up to realize that even in a communist country one life makes a difference. We pray that they will grow up to love their country and that they'll stay here and be proud of who they are."

When Faith Is Pure and Undiluted

Norman and I didn't get back to our hotel until midnight, and we were almost reeling with exhaustion. We had to get up at 3:30 A.M. to catch our flight back to London. As we crept wearily down the stairs to the registration area to check out, I looked up, and there they were—all the local pastors, their wives, their children, and their friends. Then they all began to sing, "We are one in the Spirit, we are one in the Lord."

Norman and I just stood there and cried like children because these people had made a special effort to bid us good-bye. They had worked for months on the Christian celebration, and they were exhausted. They'd gotten to bed after midnight, but they'd all gotten up and were there with their arms filled with flowers, one of which I still have pressed in my Bible as a remembrance.

Pastor Rein stepped up and said, "Never did I think that on this earth I would get such a taste of heaven."

I looked at Rein and I thought, *I'm the one who got a taste of heaven. Just being in your presence and seeing your pure, undiluted faith has burned away some of my own apathy.*

It's hard to describe the impact people have on our lives. You can drink weak orange juice for years, and it will be fine until somebody gives you a glass of the real thing. Suddenly you're startled by the intensity of the taste. I wonder sometimes whether we haven't diluted things to such an extent that they seem fine because everybody is drinking the same mediocre thing. When you suddenly come upon undiluted faith, it almost chokes you.

As our Aeroflot jet winged its way through the skies, I thought again of our friends in Estonia, and I recalled a moment from the night before. I was standing near the stage of the Lenin Cultural Auditorium after the celebration had ended, talking with Tor, the man who had translated for me, and a woman who had been an interpreter for the main speaker. KGB agents had been at the back of the hall, keeping an eye on what was being said to be sure no one was abusing any privileges. As we all stood there talking, one of the KGB men walked up to the woman interpreter and said in front of all of us in Russian, "I would like to put you in prison, and one day it will be possible again."

Then he turned on his heel and walked away. Tor quickly translated what the KGB agent had said and his woman friend asked us to stop there and pray for the KGB agent, saying, "This man needs Jesus."

There was no fear, no hatred, no arrogance. The KGB man was one of many hard-liners from the old school who didn't like what was happening one bit. Seeing Christians congregate to sing praises to God was a bitter pill for him to swallow.

That woman taught me much about how to bless and not to curse. She reminded me of what Jesus said in the Beatitudes. The happy ones are those who are persecuted and cursed and yet pray for those who persecute them. I felt at that moment that I was looking into the faces of the truly happy ones who knew their lives did make a difference.

Do We Hear Him Clapping?

Every time I think of those Estonian Christians, I am reminded of a story about a famous conductor who came from Germany to America to lead one of the greatest orchestras ever assembled. It was an incredible performance, and as the final crescendo of music died away, the audience rose to its feet, applauding and cheering. The lone exception was a man in the front row, who remained seated, refusing to clap.

The conductor came off the stage looking distressed, and someone said, "What's wrong? Listen. Listen to the applause! Listen to the cheers!"

"There is one man in the front row who isn't clapping," the conductor said.

"So what?" was the answer. "Listen to everybody else."

"You don't understand," the conductor said sadly. "That man is my teacher. He is the master."

I often ask myself, just as the conductor did, "Who is clapping?" Being a Christian means seeking applause of a different kind. If the Lord is sitting there in the front row of my life and isn't clapping, it's because I have settled for watered-down faith when I could have reached out for the real thing.

Our Choices Affect God After All

Undiluted faith is the kind that never forgets that one life does make a difference. Our choices always count. When you read the book of Job, it is not difficult for you to detect that the wisest words of advice come from Job's younger friend, the angry but sincere Elihu. He makes many telling points, to which Job has no reply. While trying to explain God's sovereign greatness, Elihu makes what he believes is a true statement:

> If you sin, it does nothing to God.
>   Even if your sins are many, they do
>   nothing to God.
> If you are good, you give nothing to God.
>   He receives nothing from your hand.
> Your evil ways only hurt a man like
>   yourself.
>   And the good you do only helps other
>   human beings. (Job 35:6–8)

Theologians will undoubtedly say that in the final analysis Elihu is right. The God All-Powerful needs nothing to sustain Him. No one would argue that, but in another very real sense Elihu is wrong. As Philip Yancey wrote, "The opening and closing . . . chapters of Job prove that God was greatly affected by the response of one man and that cosmic issues were at stake."[1]

Yancey went on to say that the "wager" between God and Satan "resolved decisively that the faith of a single human being counts for very much, indeed."[2]

To think otherwise is to fall into Satan's trap and believe that our lives and our actions don't really make a difference. Satan loves it when the Christian sales representative who struggles with pornography reaches one more time for the adult television channel while alone in his hotel room. The devil rejoices when the young woman who's tired of her marriage lies in her husband's arms, dreaming of someone else. And he rubs his hands in glee when the business-person makes out a tax return that makes it look as if he had a harder year than the prosperous one that he and his family enjoyed.

If our lives don't make a difference and we can do nothing for God, why bother? Who really cares? God is loving and forgiving. We're all human, and the Lord will understand. We can always bail out by each saying, "If my life had been easier, I'd have made better choices. I never thought it would be like this."

Every Right Choice Makes Heaven Shout

When I was a little girl my favorite story was *Peter Pan*. As I watched the movie for the first time, the words of Peter Pan rang in my ears: "Every time a child says, 'I don't believe in fairies,' a fairy dies." Later that night I lay in bed saying over and over, "I do believe in fairies, I do believe in fairies. Of course, I believe in fairies. My dog believes in fairies; my cat believes in fairies; my mum *loves* fairies."

I have to tell you that today I don't believe in fairies, but I do believe this:

> Every time a believer struggles with sorrow or loneliness or ill health or pain and chooses to trust and serve God anyhow, a bell rings out across heaven and the angels give a great shout. Why? Because one more pilgrim has shown again that he or she understands that Jesus is worth it all.

Life can be hard—and grossly unfair. When the bad things happen, we often ask, "Can I trust God?" But perhaps the real question is, "Can God trust you and me?" Can He trust us to hold on? Can He trust us to want to become mature Christians, or will we remain little children who believe in Him only if He makes it worth our while? When life seems to cave in for no reason at all, and hell is on our backs, will we hold onto heaven or not?

If we're going to be able to handle life when it doesn't seem to make sense, we have to get real. We have to set our faces in the right direction and keep walking as He walked.[3] At times the road will be long and dark, the mountains unscalable. No, we won't always make perfect choices, because we're human. Sometimes it will seem we take two steps forward and one step back, but it doesn't really matter. *All that really matters is being on the right road.*

There Is a New Emerging Leadership

I was walking through the mall the other evening, flipping through the pages of a new book I had just purchased. I became so interested I almost walked into the tiny wheelchair of a little girl who couldn't have been more than four years old. My heart ached as I looked down at that little child, and I thought, *Lord, how I wish I were the kind of person who walks so in tune with You and had such faith that I could look into the eyes of this little girl and say, "In the Name of Jesus Christ of Nazareth, rise up and walk!"*

I long to see God's power and glory strewn across people's lives rather than the wreckage and chaos that is so often there. I do believe with all my heart that a new Christian leadership is emerging during this last decade of Christianity's second millennium. These people aren't necessarily the ones with household names whose books are given glowing reviews in the magazines. They don't necessarily conduct meetings attended by huge crowds who witness miracles or signs and wonders. Nonetheless, I believe they are a new emerging leadership, because they are people who have been baptized in love, people who have had their hearts broken and who can sing with Isaac Watts:

> To Christ who won for sinners' grace
> By bitter grief and anguish sore
> Be praise from all the ransomed grace
> Forever and forevermore.[4]

You can tell when you're in the company of those who have been through deep water. They have been through the very valley of the shadow of death, but they have walked every step of the way holding onto Jesus' hand. And they have emerged on the other side, a brighter light, a more tender heart, with a loving, outstretched hand for others.

All around us in the streets of America and across this world we see devastation. We see people whose lives are broken. We look across to Communist nations and see disillusionment as their Marxist-Leninist regime has fallen apart and left a gaping void.

What will move in to fill that void? I believe and I pray with all my heart that God will so baptize His church in His love that we will learn what it means not to seek our own; that we will want to love and expect nothing in return; that we will daily come before the King of kings and the throne of grace and say:

"Lord Jesus, I can't make it through one more day without You. I just don't have enough love. When I see my reflection in the mirror, I am puzzled because I know the value You have placed on my life. I know that, through the Cross, You have proclaimed to all the world that this is what You think I'm worth. And I wear that proudly, like a new suit of clothes. I want to walk today through a world that has gone sour, bringing the fragrance of Jesus Christ wherever I go and never forgetting that just one life—even my life—can make a difference."

NOTES

1 It Wasn't Supposed to Be This Way

1. See Job 1:21.
2. Greg Nelson and Bob Farell, "God Loves You." Copyright © 1989 by Summerdawn Music/ASCAP/Greg Nelson Music (Admin. by Lorenz Creative Services)/BMI. Used by permission.
3. John Fischer, *True Believers Don't Ask Why* (Minneapolis: Bethany House Publishers, 1989), p. 19.
4. Ibid., p. 19.
5. See Romans 8:38–39.

2 No Hidden Places

1. See John 4:24.
2. Phil McHugh, "In Heaven's Eyes." Copyright © 1985, River Oaks Music Co. Used by permission.
3. Al Kasha and Joel Hirschhorn, *Reaching the Morning After* (Nashville: Thomas Nelson Publishers, 1986), p. 13.
4. Ibid., p. 153.
5. Al Kasha, "The Morning After." Copyright © 1972, W. B. Music Corp. and Warner-Tamerlane Publishing Co. Used by permission.

3 Living Sacrifices Don't Crawl Away

1. See Ephesians 5:2.

4   Be God's Friend, Not Just His Servant

1. See John 15:14–15.
2. Jon Sweet, Rod Trott, and Sheila Walsh, "Trapeze." Copyright ©
   1987, Swot Patch Music, Word Music. Used by permission.

5   Ship-Burning for Beginners: Laguna

1. Steve and Annie Chapman, "The Ships Are Burning." Copyright ©
   1990, Times and Seasons Music, Inc. Used by permission.
2. See Luke 12:48.

6   Ship-Burning for Beginners: Kauai

1. See Matthew 26:36–42; Mark 14:32–36; Luke 22:39–44.

7   Keeping It Simple Keeps It Real

1. At the time I was co-managed by Steve Lorenz and Norman.
2. See Hebrews 4:12.
3. Rod Trott and John Sweet, "Sand in the Hand." Copyright © 1986,
   Swot Patch Music. Used by permission.
4. Sheila Walsh, Greg Nelson, and Bob Farrell, "Come into His Kingdom." Copyright © 1989, Word Music, Summerdawn Music/Greg
   Nelson Music. Used by permission.
5. Sheila Walsh, "It Could Have Been Me." Copyright © 1990, Word
   Music. Used by permission.
6. Ibid.
7. See Matthew 16:24.
8. See Matthew 26:31–35.
9. See John 21:1–18.
10. See Job 33:8–9.
11. See Job 33:18.
12. See Job 34:10–12.

8   God Has Left Us a Job to Do

1. See Matthew 25:35, 40.
2. See Hebrews 13:2.
3. Rod Trott, Sheila Walsh, and Jon Sweet, "Angels with Dirty Faces."
   Copyright © 1986, Swot Patch Music. Used by permission.

9   When All of Heaven Is Silent

1. See Job 6:4.
2. See Job 13:3–4.
3. David Biebel, *If God Is Good, Why Do I Hurt So Bad?*
4. Ibid.
5. Rebecca Manley Pippert, *Hope Has Its Reasons* (New York: Harper & Row, 1989).

10   There Is a Better Song to Sing!

1. Irving Stone, *Lust for Life* (New York: Doubleday, 1934).
2. Philip Yancey, *Disappointment with God* (Grand Rapids: Zondervan Publishing House, 1988), p. 186.

11   One Life Does Make a Difference!

1. Yancey, *Disappointment with God*, p. 170.
2. Ibid.
3. See 1 John 2:6.
4. The fifth, but seldom printed, stanza to Isaac Watts's well-known hymn "When I Survey the Wondrous Cross."